From proposal to thesis

WRITING AN UNDERGRADUATE DISSERTATION

Revised edition

From proposal to thesis

WRITING AN UNDERGRADUATE DISSERTATION

Revised edition

Denis Feather

WHITE &
MACLEAN

PUBLISHING

First published as an eBook in 2013
by White & MacLean Publishing

Revised edition published as a paperback
in 2015 by White & MacLean Publishing

ISBN: 978-2-930583-47-1

Cover design: Arati Devasher
www.aratidevasher.com

Typeset in PT Serif

Printed and bound by CPI Group (UK) Ltd,
Croydon, CR0 4YY

White & MacLean Publishing
Albert Biesmanslaan 11 / 32
B-1560 Hoeilaart
Belgium

www.whiteandmaclean.eu

Dedication

I would like to dedicate this book
to my loving wife Alison, who has stood by me
throughout all my time studying, has continued to
encourage me to complete this book,
and provided me with numerous cups
of coffee and chocolate digestives.

Biography of the author

Dr Denis Feather is a senior lecturer at the University of Huddersfield's Business School in the United Kingdom, where he has taught research methods and supervised research students for the last ten years.

Acknowledgements

I would like to acknowledge my two sons, Michael and Carl, for their technical assistance; in particular Carl, who kindly took time out from his studies on game development to develop my models and tables into high-quality files. I would also like to say thank you to my daughter, Lyndsey, who stood at my shoulder and picked out numerous typographical errors.

I would like to thank two colleagues who encouraged me, and offered some of their 30 years of experience in teaching. The first is my very dear friend Frank Withey, who sadly died in 2012; he is dearly missed. The second is Howard Jackson, with whom I taught research methods for more than eight years – thank you for your thoughtful insights.

I would like to thank my good friend Kath McDermott who is a brand champion of the first edition of the book, and who offered suggestions for improvement and acted as a sounding board in relation to this, the second edition.

Finally, I would like to thank Alasdair and Fiona White, who helped me develop this book into the polished item you see before you today. Their help and advice has been invaluable. I must also thank Alasdair for providing me with the term 'student practitioner'.

Table of Contents

List of Tables

List of Figures

List of Acronyms

CRM	customer relationship marketing
EOI	examination, observation, and interview
FE	further education
FGM	focus group member
HE	higher education

Introduction

I hope that this book will guide you through the process of preparing and writing your thesis – the DOs and DON'Ts if you like. What I have written in this book is based on my experience of supervising students at all levels of study over the last decade. However, you must (in all instances) check that you are complying with your awarding institution's policies, procedures, and guidelines for the undertaking, writing, and submission of the dissertation. The purpose of this book is to walk you through some of the processes that need to be undertaken when writing an undergraduate dissertation.

I work in a business school within a university in the UK, but the route towards achieving a dissertation in other subjects is no different.

The language, style, and formatting discussed in this book is very similar to the style required by the majority of universities, colleges and other institutions. However, once again, you need to cross-reference with the guidelines provided by your own institution, as I am aware that some institutions may have changed the way their dissertation is presented and the referencing style used. You may find the language I have used to be very formal on occasions. This has been done with good reason: to show you what your institution expects from you.

Finally, in this book I use contractions (e.g. don't, I'll, won't, and so on); I do this to keep the language interesting to the reader. However, you must not use contractions in your own academic writing, as your supervisor and second marker may frown upon this style of writing.

I hope you find this book useful.

Dr Denis Feather
The Business School
University of Huddersfield
December 2014

Chapter 1: Introduction to the dissertation

What is a dissertation?

When you first receive the written or oral instruction that you have to undertake a dissertation, your first thoughts might be 'I've got to do what?' However, of all the work that you have undertaken during your time at university, this piece is the most demanding, the most exciting, and the most important.

It is the most demanding because you will need to put a lot of effort, work, time, and emotion into its preparation and construction. It is the most exciting because it allows you to show off all that you have learnt over the last three or four years of study, and because you get to pick the subject or topic you wish to research, rather than having the subject set for you. Finally, it is the most important, because it could influence the overall grade of your degree. Remember, dissertations can be weighted as a 40-credit module (or more, depending on your institution and its policies) and as such could be equal to two 20-credit modules.

What is the purpose of the dissertation?

This is a question that I am often asked by students; I am also asked whether it has any value. The answer to the second question is easy: yes, it does have value. Why does it have value? Primarily, because it is a unique piece of work, over which you have both ownership and control. Most of my students, when I

1

inform them of this, are surprised and display a degree of angst, so much so that, in fact, some often have difficulty coming up with an idea and subject on which to conduct research. Don't worry if this is where you feel you are now. It is, from my years of supervising and listening, and I mean *really* listening to my students, that I wrote this book to help guide you through the process of producing a research proposal and quality dissertation that you can be proud of. Your dissertation has additional value, in that it evidences to potential future employers that you have the ability and skills to undertake a research project, and manage it efficiently and effectively through to completion.

The dissertation has a number of purposes. From the university's perspective, the purpose of the dissertation is a means of assessing your learning, skills, and abilities: for example, to not only read and write well but to also undertake research and follow instructions. As the saying goes, 'the devil is in the detail', and it is often here (the policies, processes, format, level of reading needed to be undertaken, time, layout, presentation, proof-reading, and many other aspects that this book covers), where students tend to falter and lose marks. For example, during a discussion I had with a friend and colleague about dissertations and what he looks for, he said that he hates it when students do not conclude their thesis well; in other words, when the conclusions do not link to the research, he marks dissertations down for this poor attention to detail. I will cover this point in more detail later in the book. Nevertheless, it is these factors of assessment and criteria that you need to nail down, if you are to do well. Try to get into good research habits from the start.

To this end, the rest of this chapter sets the scene for the development of the thesis as a whole. It outlines the processes that you will be going through, and what it is you need to attend to throughout the dissertation journey. Keep in mind that each chapter in the thesis should be written in an academic report format; that is, with numbered headings and sub-headings.

Headings and sub-headings in the first chapter

Below you will find the headings you need to include in the first chapter of your dissertation:

- Title
- Introduction to the study
- Background
- Research question
- Aim and objectives
- Rationale for the study
- Précis of the following chapters

Let's discuss these in a little more detail.

Title

The first thing you will need to come up with is a workable title for your proposed study. This is probably one of the most difficult tasks you will ever be asked to do (Quinlan, 2011), primarily because in the past the titles for your assignments have been provided for you. However, here you will really need to put your thinking cap on, and reflect upon those areas that interest you. A good place to start is to list the areas of interest you have at home (for example, music, sport, films, fashion, computers, gaming, or whatever) for which you have a real passion. By this, I mean those hobbies or interests about which you collect material, artefacts, or information. I usually suggest to my students to select five different areas of interest, and then to consider how they can apply the different concepts and theories of their studied subject to these interests. Why do I do this? It's simple. If your first idea bears no fruit, then you can revert to your second idea; in strategic management, this is what is often referred to as 'contingency planning'. This is apt here because you are thinking strategically about how you can undertake research on something that is of interest to you, and to your potential readership.

To provide you with a couple of examples, one of my business students was really interested in fishing and competed within the sport, but felt that it was viewed as an 'old man's sport'. To this end, he was looking at the perceptions of fishing as a sport, and how media could be used to change its image. Another student was very passionate about advertising and wished to look at how new media might be affecting advertising via traditional streams, such as television.

Whatever your title is, it needs to be short and to the point. Remember, this is only a working title, and will not become solid until you hand in your dissertation (see Chapter 3).

Introduction to the study

Here you should be identifying what it is you are wishing to study and why. In this section, there will be some repetitiveness, but do not be too concerned as you can tighten it up later. The main point is to get your ideas down on paper. Here you should have two or three sentences identifying the study and what it is you intend to address; in other words, the problem or question you wish to explore.

Background

This is like a mini literature review, and looks at the current thinking on the subject or topic you are interested in researching. In reality, this should be no more than 300-500 words in length as it is only the background – you will expand upon this in the literature review chapter.

Research question

It is important that you identify what your research question is, as this will then enable you to offer a tight aim and relevant objectives. Where does the research question come from? Well, it starts with an idea. The idea can come from reading around something you are interested in, an observation, or via conversations with your friends. As Roberts (2010: p.136) writes: "A question well stated is a question half answered." To this end the research question should be succinct and to the point. I often ask my students to write their research question in 35 words or less. Remember what I wrote earlier: there is likely to be some overlap and possible repetition; this is expected.

If you are undertaking a quantitative study, you may instead develop a set of hypotheses you wish to test. However, although most authors on thesis writing infer that you have either a research question or hypotheses, I would suggest writing a research question, as this will enable you to keep focused on what it is you are endeavouring to understand. Roberts (2010) suggests that the research question becomes the 'purpose statement' in a quantitative study, and that it tends to be generic, whereas the hypotheses are built around this purpose statement. The two approaches could be worded as either:

- 'This study aims to understand what is meant by the term "Academic Identity"... ' (qualitative and mixed-method approach).

or

- 'The purpose of this study is to determine what variables influence the definition of the term "Academic Identity" using a number of hypotheses.'

On hypotheses, Buckingham and Saunders (2004: p.4) write:

> Hypotheses are statements about what our theoretical propositions lead us to expect to find. They enable theories to be tested by predicting patterns of observations that should occur. Hypotheses therefore predict patterns of association in observed data as a means for testing causal theories.

The point here is that you need to be clear in what it is you are wishing to understand, and how you are going to strategically bring about a successful conclusion to your findings via the use of different research philosophies, research paradigms, and research data collection methods.

Aim and objectives

The aim of the study is to rework your research topic/question so that it focuses more on what it is you are trying to understand (as a norm, this usually comes from your research title). It is usually stretched out into a sentence or two; for example: 'The aim of this study is to consider the effects of new media advertising on traditional media, such as television. This will be considered from the customers'/viewers' perspective.' See further information on this in Chapter 3.

The objectives should be drawn up to address any gaps or questions you have identified from your literature review (see Chapter 4) and in relation to your subject/topic goal. Five objectives are the norm; in Chapter 3 I have provided action words that you should use when writing your objectives.

When writing objectives you should be remembering the acronym of SMART – Specific, Measurable, Achievable, Realistic, and Timely (Robson, 2002; Saunders et al., 2007; Oliver, 2010; Quinlan, 2011). Initially focus on 'Specific' and 'Measurable', and then 'Achievable' followed by 'Timely'. Specific is the most important because objectives need to be short and to the point. Lastly, they should be 'Realistic'. This means that you can achieve them and as such, they are not too ambitious. I would change this acronym to SMARTS, the last 'S' standing for 'Stretching'. The objectives should stretch you so that you learn, but not overstretch you so that you cannot accomplish the task because the objectives become unrealistic and you cannot meet your goal. Remember, at undergraduate level, you are not trying to reinvent the wheel, but you do want to offer research that can be added to the pot of knowledge in your subject.

Some universities are now encouraging their undergraduate students to publish from their dissertation work. You will need to check with your own institution if this is the case. But if they do, and your work is of a standard, I would strongly recommend that you consider this, as it will offer you a further competitive advantage when you come to look to securing a full-time position in the career of your choice, or if you wish to study further.

Rationale for the study

This is relatively easy to produce and comprises of answering four basic questions:

1. Why are you undertaking this research?

2. What is the new knowledge that you will bring to the table?

3. What is the motivation behind you undertaking this study?

4. Who do you think will be interested in reading your research and its findings?

The answers to these four bullet points should be no more than one sentence in length; I have seen pages written on this, and it really is not necessary.

All the above should also appear in your proposal, most of which will then be incorporated, rephrased and expanded upon in your main thesis. If you do take a direct lift from your proposal to include in your dissertation, do not forget to '***self reference***'; you do not wish to be suspected of 'self-plagiarising'. You will need to look at the referencing pack and policy on academic integrity provided by your institution on how to self reference and subsequently how to avoid being brought up for the lack of academic integrity. With the current rise in the practice of plagiarism, academics and universities are now bringing into force more stringent penalties. So my advice is don't do it; it really isn't worth it.

Précis of the following chapters

This is where the first chapter in your dissertation changes from your proposal. At this point, you will offer a quick overview or précis of what the following chapters will be covering. For example:

> Chapter 2: Literature Review: Here I will discuss the different concepts and theories I identified in my dissertation proposal, and will compare, contrast, and critique different authors' viewpoints on these concepts/theories.

> Chapter 3: Methodology: Here I will outline the philosophies and methods I have employed in order to conduct the research that answers the aim and objectives of the study. It can be seen that I adopted a mixed-method approach to my research and a mixed-paradigm approach using interpretivism and positivism – interpretivism being the dominant philosophy as I wished to gain people's perceptions of how they saw new media impacting on the future of television advertising.

> Chapter 4: Findings/results

> Chapter 5: Discussion

> Chapter 6: Conclusions and recommendations

This then concludes Chapter 1 of the thesis. Remember this chapter sets the scene for the following chapters and for your study. Do not forget to keep signposting back to this chapter (when relevant) to aid the reader in their understanding of what it is you are trying to accomplish with your work. Further, in Chapter 3, it might be prudent to present your aim and objectives once more, as it will have been some time since your reader first became aware of them in Chapter 1.

Now let's look at some of the processes that you need to keep in mind when writing your dissertation and its subsequent chapters. You may need to refer back to these from time to time, to ensure you are not drifting from the task you are currently working on.

Length of the dissertation

The standard length of an undergraduate dissertation is usually between 12,000 and 15,000 words. '**Oh my God!**' I hear you cry. Try not to think about the word count; instead, focus on the quality of your written work. Again, I hear you say, 'Easy for you to say'. That's fine. Instead, try to think of it as six assignments, each comprising of 2,000-2,500 words. Breaking it down into manageable chunks like this will make the task more achievable. However, not all chapters will be the same length; some chapters will be shorter than others and it is the total word count that matters. Where chapters (such as Chapter 1) might be shorter, the words you do not use there can be employed elsewhere, thus allowing you to drill deeper on a particular discussion.

What your institution requires

As I identified earlier, you will also need to familiarise yourself thoroughly with your institution's dissertation guidelines. Why do I write this? Simply, it is so that you can start preparing the format of your dissertation in advance, and to familiarise yourself with the processes that they wish you to comply with. You should have been given these guidelines by the module leader for the dissertation, or by your supervisor. If you do not have them, ask for them; you need this important documentation to enable you to undertake the task. Also, ensure that you also have a copy of the marking criteria (if it is not included in the module booklet) as you need to know the standard and expectations that your institution is requiring you write to, and comply with. The last thing you want is to get to the end of the journey and find out that there is a section of the marking criteria where you have not obtained a grade, thus losing valuable points. You should be constantly referring back to these criteria throughout your time in writing up both your proposal and your dissertation.

Order of writing

The next thing you need to plan is the order of the writing you will have to undertake. I have provided you with the chapter order (see above), but it is unlikely you will write the chapters in this order.

The first thing to write is the 'research proposal'. In most institutions, this will be assessed and graded before you are allowed to start on the dissertation proper. Other institutions may not bother with a proposal. In either case, I think a proposal is essential. The proposal gives you the opportunity to test your idea, and provides your supervisor with a valuable insight to your capabilities, skills, and level of writing, and if any are found wanting, they can then recommend training programmes for you to attend. As such, the proposal is the plan of what you intend to research and why. It will help you clarify in your own mind exactly what it is you are trying to achieve.

Literature review

The literature review is the next piece of writing (and, to be truthful, is part of the first piece of writing) as it is from the literature that you read that you will acquire your ideas. Additionally, you will need to write a small review in your proposal that covers at least one theory or concept (as you cannot cover them all there), which, again, evidences the depth of reading you are currently working to, and will help your supervisor identify if you need to widen your reading.

When writing the literature review for the proposal, I suggest to students to commence with an introductory sentence that goes something like this:

> For the purpose of the proposal, it is obvious that a full literature review cannot be undertaken. However, the concepts and theories one intends to cover in the main thesis are academic identity, professionalism, scholarship, identity, culture, and marketisation. From these concepts and theories, the subject of academic identity will be used to offer the reader a brief overview of what this concept is and how different authors suggest different views on this subject.

Today (and from my own experiences), students tend to look to the Internet for the information they require. This practice will not be sufficient to get you the depth of knowledge you need: you will need to read books and journal articles (which I cover in later chapters) in order to gain this knowledge. Many students use Wikipedia; this is poor practice and many institutions will not accept Wikipedia as an academically acceptable reference source. Of course, you can use this tool to give you an insight, but look to sources that are more credible when formulating your discussions and supporting the evidence you put forward. I for one (and I know from talking with other lecturers that they do too) start to question the strength of an argument in a student's work when they use this site to support their discussions.

Another trend I have noticed recently is the use of dictionaries creeping into the main body of text and in the bibliography. Although these are more credible than Wikipedia, they should not be really used as a principal reference within the main text at this level of study. One would expect this of A-level students, but not final-year students on a degree programme. When endeavouring to define something, look first to the textbooks, better still the journal articles, as it is here that you will obtain contemporary views, which will give you the opportunity to possibly critique a point. Remember I said that this assessment is probably one of the most important you will have to undertake in your time at university, therefore do not adopt a poor work ethos now. You have worked hard to get to this point.

Questionnaire

The next piece of writing you will undertake will be to develop your questionnaire or interview schedule, depending on whether the stance you are taking is quantitative or qualitative. If you are applying a mixed-method approach, you may have to develop both. The development and piloting of questionnaires are covered in Chapter 5 on methodology. However, it is advisable to study some questionnaires to get ideas about question formats and layout. Most students today tend to use an electronic questionnaire, which I would recommend, as the hard work is done for you: all you have to do is type the question and identify what type of question you wish to pose, that is, open-ended or closed questions, Likert scales, opinion questions, etc. You can also now add different themes to your questionnaire to make it more appealing to the respondent. Some useful sites to try are Google Docs, Toluna QuickSurveys, KwikSurveys, and there are many more. However, be careful, as some sites have a charge, or a limitation on how many you can send out, or have returned.

Remember, your supervisor may have to sign off your questionnaire before you can make it live and send it out to your target audience. There could be two reasons for this. One, you are seen as an ambassador of your university, so the university's reputation could come into disrepute if you send out a poor questionnaire that is not well thought through. Two, your university might have a research ethics form that you have to complete. This is where you may have to fill out sections and then sign the document to say you have, and intend to, comply with research ethical guidelines set by your university and/or professional body. A recommended book, seen by many academics as a must-read, is Oppenheim's book *Questionnaire Design, Interviewing and Attitude Measurement*; it is a heavy read, but invaluable in its insights.

Writing up the methodology

You can also commence writing up your methodology, once your proposal has been graded and approved and whilst working on other chapters. At this point you cannot write up the findings and results chapter, as you will not have your data collected yet. This means that the remaining chapters, Chapters 5 and 6, cannot be written at this time. Therefore, it is important that you start collecting your primary data as soon as practicably possible – and that means three to four months before the hand-in date.

Finally, the dissertation is your responsibility and ownership is yours. I can guide you if you let me, but I cannot make you sit down to read or write. If you are serious about obtaining a good grade, and wish to succeed, you will do this. However, you need to want this badly enough. The same goes for your supervisor: if you do not visit them, and obtain formative feedback on drafts, they cannot be held responsible. *You* are the driver of this, not your supervisor.

Your 30-second recap

I've provided you with an overview of what a dissertation is, its purpose, and what you need to accomplish in order to give yourself a chance at success.

I've introduced you to what must be present in the first chapter of your dissertation and provided you with key headings, under which all you need to do is write your research story.

I've indicated the importance of reading relevant and credible material in relation to your research idea. Reading has become a dirty word to some students, but it is the only way you are going to gain the knowledge you need to enable you to understand, which you then can apply to the problem at hand.

Chapter 2: Don't worry – help is at hand

Student practitioner

I would hazard a bet that you have never viewed yourself as a practitioner, but if you think about it, you have spent the last three to four years becoming just that – a practitioner.

What is it I am practising, you might ask. Well, for a start, you began your first year practising how to interpret what your different lecturers were requiring in order for you to obtain a good grade on your individual or group assessments. From that, you then started to practise reading different material to what you did at school or college, and to a completely new level. You practised how to write well, to structure your arguments, and not to be descriptive (which I no doubt guess many of you have had written on your assignment at some time).

In year two, you practised even more. You practised new skills: for example, to think critically, to present, to hold discussions in class, and even to reflect. Urgh! I know reflection is not a word many students like; however, in academia, management or the working environment per se, this practice is very useful. When you think about it, you reflect every day without actually giving it a second thought, the difference being you are not writing it down. Without you being aware of it, we as lecturers have been guiding you (even though you may not be consciously aware of it), on how to become self-autonomous learners, where you develop the skills to find material for yourself.

Now, I am going to get you to practise something else: keeping a research journal.

Research journal

I can hear you ask: What do I need one of those for? Well, because it is a researcher's craft tool – in fact it is one of the most useful tools when it comes to reflecting on what you have done and recollecting your thoughts. Remember, you cannot remember everything, so why not keep a journal. You never know, you might even enjoy it! Many of my second-year students have commented on how they have enjoyed collecting artefacts, and recording information on how they found certain information; more importantly, how they went about finding that information, and how to find it again, if needs be.

If you have watched *Indiana Jones and the Last Crusade*, you will no doubt believe that the film was all about the search for the Holy Grail. For me, it was about his father's research journal and the notes contained within it. It contained his father's reflections, instructions, diagrams, notes, maps, his observations, and all manner of things useful to his research on the Holy Grail and how to find it.

Your research title is your version of the Holy Grail so, like the elder Dr Jones, you need to keep copious notes, diagrams, and other artefacts that will prompt your memory when the time comes to write up your ideas.

Your research journal should be as useful as Dr Jones' was to him. You should note down all titles, authors, and other essential data for the sources to be referenced, together with the page on which you found the idea, diagram, or quote. Furthermore, if your university uses the American Psychological Association (APA) 6th referencing format, you will need to record the Digital Object Identifier (DOI) because it is needed in the bibliography part of your thesis.

I suggest you also record in your research diary when you read a particular piece, when you accessed a particular online source (and give its exact URL). Record the arguments you may encounter, and also the counter-arguments (and where to find them again). Indeed, record every step you take in your research so that you can re-trace your steps if needed.

Let's take a closer look at this.

Five ideas

When you commence your research, write down five topics or ideas (see Figure 2.1) of what you would like to research. Then do some reading around these ideas to test their feasibility. In other words, can I get data on the topic, what are the core concepts surrounding the topic, would I be able to get my questionnaires to, or obtain interviews with, those people who fall into my target sample?

Taking notes, recording citations and references

Another useful aspect of the research journal is that you can take notes from papers you have read, either online or offline. Visit http://wac.colostate.edu/journal/vol16/boch.pdf (Boch and Piolat, 2005), and http://www.citewrite.qut.edu.au/about/QUTcitewrite-2010_templates.PDF (QUT, 2008). You should *always* record in your journal the full citation from where you obtained the data. For example, one of my students found a good piece of evidence online, which supported the research she was undertaking, but forgot to record the full citation. When she tried to find it again, it was no longer there and she could not find it. This meant that she only had the author's name and the year of publication for a reference within the main text, but was unable to provide the full citation needed for her bibliography.

Figure 2.1 Five research ideas.

When you read articles, you should take notes from these articles and then summarise them in your own words. By doing this, you will have read it once and taken notes, but will have then read it again to summarise the article. This is referred to as reinforcing your learning. This practice (see I told you that you were a practitioner) will give you the necessary knowledge you need to start to formulate an argument in your discussions.

A practical guide to organising your life as a researcher and writer

Research, write, correct, edit, proofread – five steps to success

You may ask why I am placing this here and not at the end of the book. It is simple really: the sooner you learn these different processes and get into good habits, the more they will become second nature. Moreover, most students become fed-up with looking at their dissertation when it gets close to handing it in. As such, many tell me they do not feel like going through it again to proofread it. This is sad, and my students do not get away with it. Think about it: you have just spent most of the last year undertaking reading, collecting primary data, analysing that data, and putting together a discussion and conclusion that addresses a problem you have identified. Surely, you would now want to submit something that is as error-free as possible. I know you will have a number of other assignments for different modules on the go at the same time, and that is why the quicker you learn to correct, edit, and proofread as you go, the easier it will be when you come to the end of the journey.

Bear in mind that you need to leave sufficient time for editing and you will need to proofread your draft thesis at least twice (Swetnam, 2000), possibly even three or more times if you have a learning disability such as dyslexia. If this latter point is a case in question for you, you will need to be working with your dyslexia tutor and the learning development group/academic support tutors (depending on what your institutions refers to them as). Nevertheless, all of you will need to proofread/copy-edit in order to eradicate any mistakes, and then you will need to think about the format. Is it in the format your institution has asked for? Check your module or dissertation booklet that was given to you to ensure you are complying with your university's guidelines on the submission of undergraduate dissertations.

Plan your time: you do not want to stumble at the last hurdle. I discovered an excellent book that not only helped me with my writing, but also in planning out what I am going to write, how to go about proofreading and copy-editing, and which makes grammar really easy to understand. The book is by Alex Osmond and is entitled *Academic writing and grammar for students*.

A time for writing

Different people have different ways of working. I have known some students who write a little bit at a time, go away from it, and then return later to complete it. The problem with this is that they have to re-read what they have written in order to remind themselves of what they had already covered, and then pick up the thread of thought and run with it. The time taken to re-read and collect one's thoughts is time-consuming; time which could be better spent on writing. Try instead to write in sections, so that when you return to the work you are commencing a new section, and you do not have to read the previous sections as you know you had completed them. The idea here is to get your thoughts down on paper; you can edit when the section is complete.

I have also known students burn the midnight oil; some staying all night in the library to get the thesis finished in time for the hand-in date – in some instances that very morning. This, again, is not good practice. If you are tired, you will not be able to offer clarity of thought; you need to come to your writing fresh and in the correct mindset, determined to finish the next section or sections.

When it comes to the way of writing, nobody knows you like you do. However, reflect on your current practices, so that you can consider whether your current practice is helping you to be efficient and effective with your time for writing and how you write. Alternatively, consider whether your current practices are in fact a hindrance to you. It is best to sort them now, rather than when it is too late and there is no time left.

Comfort zone

Most of us prefer to write where our materials are at hand and in the comfort of our own little sanctuary, wherever that may be. For me, it is in my armchair, with my laptop and my books and journals around me – much to the annoyance of my wife. I also like to listen to heavy rock music when I'm writing; in fact, I'm doing this right now whilst writing this chapter. I've read that some psychologists believe that you need to stimulate both sides of your brain to write at your best. Having said that, I'm not sure that nodding my head in time with my favourite group AC/DC is conducive to getting my ideas down on paper, in a clear and coherent manner. However, it does get me pumped up and ready to write, which works for me. Find out what works for you, and do it.

Other people prefer to write in solitude, in total quiet, which is fine. One of my dissertation students informed me that this is how she prefers to work; for her, her comfort zone was in her bedroom. Another student informed me that he preferred to work in the library late at night, when there were hardly any students around and it was very quiet. He stated that he sometimes liked to walk away from his desk and sit on one of the couches near to where he was working, and then go back to his laptop and write some more; go back to the couch, reflect, and then come back – weird, I know, but it worked for him and that is all that matters. Both students were my dissertation students, and both students obtained high grades. As Saunders et al. (2009: p.521) so rightly points out: 'One person's distractions are another person's necessities.' From this it is quite evident that whatever you find distracts you from being your most productive needs to be removed post haste.

Writer's toolkit

One of the writer's main tools is his or her brain. You need to think, and in order to accomplish this you need to have the necessary tools to capture your thoughts. I have already discussed the research journal, where you should capture your observations and take notes or keep artefacts. However, today, more and more people are communicating on the go, using Twitter™, Facebook™, LinkedIn™, or other forms of social media. When it comes to writing your dissertation, you need to be disciplined and firm with yourself. Therefore, switch off Facebook and any other form of communication when you are trying to both think and write. Recollect what I said earlier about being in the right mindset, and that expressing one's thoughts on paper is harder than verbal communication. Allow yourself the space to do this.

Having said this, mobile phones and iPads now have the means to record on the go. If you observe something, or think of something that is relevant to your research, record a message to yourself so you can revisit it later, or save it as a file on your computer to revisit when the time comes. The point being, there should be no excuse for not capturing your thoughts. I remember a time when they used to say (and still do), keep a pen and paper beside your bed as you are more often likely to have thoughts on your projects whilst you are asleep. If you are anything like me, you are more likely to knock the pen off, whilst trying to grasp it in a semi-conscious state. It might be better to record your thoughts; after all, most of us keep our mobile phones at the side of our bed. Wow, we are a sad lot!

Computers are wondrous tools; they allow us the scope to produce something useful, or something that is absolute rubbish. Do not produce the latter.

Abandon all hope, ye that do not save their data

It never ceases to amaze me how many times we, as lecturers, tell you, the student, to save your work on different sources – CDs, pen-drives, portable hard drives, computer hard drives, possibly even on your account at your institution where they set aside space for you to do this, and which is backed up every night. However, not all institutions may have this facility, so check with your supervisor or student IT support person first. 'Cloud' is another alternative, but this is down to personal preference; some people love it, others hate it.

Do not rely on the computer saving your work regularly. I know it is set to do this (usually the default is every ten minutes), but make it a habit to click on 'save' every few minutes, and when you have finished, save your work to multiple sources as indicated above. Even put a copy in the Cloud (if you use this resource); that way you can download it to any of your devices. However, if you have sensitive material or data, do not store this in the Cloud. In addition, bear in mind the Data Protection Acts of the countries in which you are studying; there will be some differences, but the bottom line is the same: keep your data safe, and protect it with a password, even your pen drive. Only last year, I learnt of an incident from a colleague, where a student had had to rush off to the toilet (now behave yourself, keep your mind on track), leaving their pen drive in the computer, and the screen open. It was not until the student had been brought before the Academic Integrity Officer for possible plagiarism that they learned that the student sitting at the computer next to them, was undertaking a similar assignment, had reached down, removed the pen drive, copied its contents to their pen drive, and returned the original to the USB slot. Although the student who had to dash off did not commit plagiarism, they were given a lesser penalty for not protecting their data, and allowing others the opportunity to access it, with or without their knowledge. So please, be very careful with your data.

Take note: if you lose your data from not saving it regularly or to different devices and formats, your institution might not be sympathetic. Most institutions make it a policy, which is usually written in the *Student's Handbook*, that it is the student's responsibility to keep multiple copies. As a result, extensions may not be given under this guideline. As lecturers, and I think I can speak for most of us, we do not like to see our students upset, and it upsets us when we are powerless to help. Therefore, it is in your best interest if you get into the habit of saving your work regularly, and to multiple devices and/or sources.

When should I write?

The question of when you should write is really down to you. I have discussed that people have their different comfort zones and how they prefer to work, but not when. Every person has a certain time during the day when they are at their most creative. For example, mine is at home, usually on a Saturday or Sunday morning, before the family get up and commence their daily routines. However, necessity means that sometimes I have to write in the evenings when I get home. One colleague I talked with said that the best time for him was in the afternoon; another said the mornings during the week, and that he turned off anything that might distract him – phones, e-mail, etc.

Time management

There are numerous books on time management and, in my opinion, having read a number of them and also having attended some training sessions on this subject, if you were to practise everything that is suggested, you would never get anything done. This is because you will have spent most of your time undertaking the tasks they suggest you do in order to remember what you have to do and when. Nevertheless, time cannot be retrieved; once it is lost, it is lost forever. You can never gain it back, unless you cut corners, which I ***definitely do not*** recommend you do in any situation. However, it does mean that you will have to rob time from another task or tasks (sort of like taking from Peter to pay Paul, as the old proverb goes), to allow you to complete both. At the end of the day, poor planning from the beginning means that maybe two pieces of work are jeopardised due to (sorry, there is no other way of saying this) laziness on the part of the student. Therefore, the practice of managing your time is crucial.

Time management on the go

Most students today have state-of-the-art mobile telephones, iPads, or laptops, so why not set time aside in your calendar, with a tone to remind you, that the writing time for your dissertation is approaching and that you need to be there at your desk or wherever, ready to start. Again, you could make this a standard practice in your calendar, as you will have identified what time of day is best for you to write, and where. Moreover, remember to inform your friends that you will not be available at those times. I will not lie to you: this is not an easy thing to do. You need to remember that you have spent time, effort, and a lot of money to get to this point in your studies. Do not throw it away now because friends want you to go out or because you cannot be bothered to get out of bed. You chose to undertake your course of study for a reason; stand firm on that conviction and the goal you have set yourself for your future career choice.

How much should I write?

Saunders et al. (2009: p.520) argue that for most people it is possible to write 2,000 words a day; this (in theory) is not too unrealistic. However, from my years of experience, when I have asked students to prepare a draft of 2,000 words and given them a week to submit it to me, I get the impression I have asked the impossible. You would think I had just hit them with a wet fish! They argue that 2,000 words are too many to produce in that time and I do not exaggerate here. I have had students who have had an assignment brief for a whole year, where the assignment word count was 2,500, and the student has come and asked (a week before the deadline) if they can have an extension for whatever reason. Does the above narrative sound familiar? Do you know a friend who has done this? Have you done this? If yes, then I rest my case, as my argument is proven and shows that you must set aside time to write.

A friend of mine reminded me that, as students, you often write around 800 words per question in an examination situation. If you have three questions to answer, it might be that you write 800 for the first question, 600 for the second, and possibly around 500 for the last, equating to 1,900 words in two hours. Therefore, it is possible to write a large number of words in a relatively short space of time. However, remember that, with the dissertation, what we as lecturers are looking for is quality over quantity.

It is better to write around 500 words a day, rather than writing none. To give you a further example, another student of mine was so anxious about producing good quality writing, which was well within her capacity, that she became focused on the fact that anything she wrote would be rubbish. As a result, despite me and other lecturers guiding her, she did not listen, and thus produced nothing. She spent so much time seeking others' opinions and reassurances that she got herself very confused, resulting in being afraid to commit anything to paper. This is a good example of both anxiety and information overload. If you are anxious about writing or undertaking the dissertation, speak with your supervisor, who is there to help you, not hinder you. If you are afraid of committing your thoughts to paper, produce drafts of 500 words for your supervisor to look at. However, please, do not leave it to the end and expect supervisors to look at drafts at the 'eleventh hour' before submitting your proposal or your thesis. They will just not have the time, and nor will you if there any corrections that need doing.

To help you with your time management, your Gantt chart (see Figure 5.3 in Chapter 5) should be placed near your computer so you can see if you are falling behind. Check with your supervisor to ascertain if you are making the progress they are expecting. I am sure they will tell you very quickly if you are not.

Meeting with your supervisor

Once you know who your supervisor is, be proactive and make an appointment to meet with him or her. Remember they are very busy people and you are not the only student they are likely to be supervising. The sooner you meet with them, the more likely it is that you will get a time and a regular day to see each other that is convenient to you both. Furthermore, your supervisor is not on call 24/7; they have a home life too, so do not expect them to be at your disposal. Arrange and confirm further appointments if you need to. If you cannot keep an appointment, do not be thoughtless and leave your supervisor waiting for you; e-mail or telephone them to let them know if you are not going to attend. They will thank you for this, as it will allow them to undertake other work that needs doing.

Ask your supervisor how she or he prefers to work: do they like hard draft copies, or do they prefer to receive a draft e-mailed to them? Via e-mail means they can use 'track changes' and send it back to you. This then may free them up to discuss issues that are more important with you at your meeting, or answer any questions you may have. Many supervisors are allotted a specific amount of time for seeing each student; for example, the institutions I have worked at have varied between 15 and 20 minutes per student and only so many visits per academic year. Therefore, you will need to make the most of the time you have with your supervisor.

Professionalism: editing, copy-editing, and proofreading – forget these at your peril!

Before you send your supervisor any work, ensure that you have checked it for spelling and grammatical errors. If you have learning difficulties, such as dyslexia, ensure your supervisor is made aware of it and that you use any software that you have at your disposal to help you. In addition, you can see the academic skills tutors or learning development tutors. Different institutions have different names for these people, but these staff members will (if you make an appointment) read your draft for errors and offer advice. It is not your supervisor's role to do this for you; they are there to guide you through the process, keep you on track, and play 'devil's advocate' to make you think and reflect. I refer you again to the book by Alex Osmond; you will really find this text very useful. If your library does not have a copy, ask if they can obtain a copy for you via the 'inter-library loan' system that most libraries use.

Another aspect of the dissertation is that your individual institution will have a set format for presenting the finished thesis. Ensure you have a copy of the format that the final submission is to be in, and that you comply with any instructions – presentation is also part of the weighting for the marking criteria at many, if not all, institutions. With this, you are evidencing that you can follow 'simple' instructions and comply with regulations; these skills are valuable to employers, even though they seem basic at first glance.

Binding

Your institution will have quite specific criteria on how your final thesis should be bound and submitted. Again, you need to comply with this request. Some institutions are happy with simple spiral binding (this is the strongest and what I would recommend if this were the case). Others like a more formal-looking thesis (which looks brilliant and something you can be proud of when it comes back) in black buckram with gold leaf lettering; but this has become expensive for students, which may be one reason why some institutions have moved to spiral or other bindings.

Although at this point in the writing process, binding is possibly the last thing you are thinking about, you need to remember that you will not be the only student looking to bind their dissertation before handing it in, so get it in for binding as soon as you can. Additionally, there might be a lead-time for the binding of dissertations, especially with black buckram; this can be anything up to three weeks or more. Start enquiring nearer the time – about three months before the hand-in date is usually a good starting point. You can then start to forward plan.

Referencing

Throughout this guide I use and provide examples of Harvard referencing. I make no apologies for this, especially when at times the writing may be seen by some as a little stiff and too academic; this is intentional. The point is that you will have a working example of how to use references, different types of quotes (those comprising of less than two lines and those comprising of two or more lines), and how to use references at the beginning, in the middle, and at the end of the sentences. It may save you some time by not having to flip between different pieces of paper or online articles. However, you will need to check that this is still in line with your institution's preferred way of referencing. Having said this, the norm now has shifted in that if the quote is 40 words or less it remains in quotation marks and if it is more than 40 words then it is indented from both sides by 1cm, single-lined spaced, and appears in a size 10 font. Again, you will need to check the formatting style guide of your institution.

A further point I would like to make you aware of is that many universities are moving to the American Psychological Association (APA) 6th Edition. Your own institution will have guidelines on how to reference in this style correctly. There are also other versions available on the Internet from other institutions; for example, I often use the style guide produced by the University of Chester, as this is a comprehensive and easy-to-use guide. Alternatively, you can also purchase the full guide from the American Psychological Association themselves, but this can be expensive.

Your 30-second recap

You're seen as a student practitioner.

You're coming up with research ideas.

I've shown you how to manage your time.

Remember to find your writing time and writing place.

Don't forget the importance of discussing things with your supervisor.

I've also talked about the quantity you should try to write.

Remember to copy-edit and proofread your work.

Don't forget to plan the binding of your thesis.

Reference correctly.

In the next chapter, I'll look at getting you started with the first leg of the journey: the proposal.

Chapter 3: A journey of a thousand miles ... starts with the proposal

Why should I write a proposal?

If this is the first time you have undertaken a dissertation, you may feel a little intimidated (White, 2000) and anxious at the idea of producing a proposal. Do not worry, this is normal; the more you read around the subject you have chosen, the more comfortable you will begin to feel. Nevertheless, you may be asking yourself 'Why do I need to write a proposal?' Well, the first and obvious reason is that it is often part of the summative assessment of the dissertation, and carries a weight equal to 20% of the overall grade for the dissertation module (although this may be different at other universities). The second reason is that it is a very important process for you to undertake, which 'makes you think carefully about what you want to do' (White, 2000). Additionally, it allows you and your supervisor the opportunity to appreciate what it is you are attempting to accomplish with your research. As Walliman (2005: p.69) writes:

> Not only is this the main opportunity to crystallize your thoughts before you embark on the project, it is also a sober consideration of how much you will be able to achieve within the few weeks/months allowed.

What is a proposal?

Basically, this is a considered description of what it is you wish to accomplish with your research, and '...how you intend to carry out the work involved till [sic] its completion' (Walliman, 2005: p.68). To this end, a proposal is:

> ...a summary of the work you have to do for the dissertation. It outlines the aims, methods, and other features of the work...It includes a statement as to the nature and purpose of the study, together with some account of the background of the subject. (White, 2000: p.68)

Now remember, at the undergraduate level you are not expected to produce the same depth of discussions that a master's or PhD student would. However, you are expected to produce useful insights into your chosen subject area by the careful and relevant application of research theory and methods. The proposal is relatively condensed; it is only 1,500-2,000 (2,500 for some institutions) words in length. As such, a great deal of thought and time needs to be put into its production in order to cover the necessary elements required to convey what it is you are attempting to accomplish.

The elements of a proposal may include:

- Title
- Introduction
- Background
- Rationale for study
- Defining the research question
- Aim and objectives
- Literature review
- Methodology: philosophies/paradigms to be adopted and why:

- whether the research is quantitative, qualitative, or a mixed-method approach;

- sampling method(s) and sample size;

- questionnaire design – structured, semi-structured, or unstructured;

    • postal, electronic, or undertaken by the researcher face-to-face with participants;

    • piloting;

    • pre-coding/post-coding;

- interview schedule design;

- offer an indication on the reliability and validity of the research to be undertaken;

- give an indication of how you intend to reduce research bias;

- data analysis (quantitative) – how the data will be analysed: PASW (Predictive Analytics SoftWare) or Excel;

- data analysis (qualitative) – how the data from interviews will be analysed: NU:DIST, NVivo, thematic, descriptive;

- possible limitations to the study;

- highlight the research ethical guidelines you intend to comply with (identify that you are aware of any ethical forms you need to have completed and signed by your supervisor before you commence your primary research);

- suggestion of the timeframe for the study – cross-sectional, or longitudinal, usually depicted in the form of a Gantt chart;

• Bibliography;

• Appendices.

Title

This is where you will need to sit and really think about what it is you wish to study; it should be something you are passionate about, which will drive and motivate you over the time period you have been allotted to complete the study. From this you will need to develop a title that will be succinct (see Quinlan, 2011), and uses only a few words to summarise your entire study, for example one of my past student's dissertation title was: *The Effects of New Media on the Future of Television Advertising*. Remember this will remain flexible, and will only be a working title until you have finished your research, at which time you will be able to tweak and finalise your title so that it reflects your completed study. This is *important*; the working title (as I stated earlier) should be one that keeps you interested and motivated for the period of the study.

Introduction

In this section, you need to introduce your reader to the study, and what it is you are aiming to achieve by undertaking the research. This may comprise of just one paragraph, but will help set the scene for the rest of the study and the thesis to come in the future.

Background

You should not assume that the reader of your proposal knows the subject area you are researching; similarly, you should not insult their intelligence. Therefore, your background should inform the reader about '...the context of the project and where it fits in with current thinking' (Walliman, 2005: p.71). A good background will also show your supervisor that you have read around your subject area. This is achieved via a small literature review (so to speak) on what different authors are currently writing about in relation to the chosen study. In other words, what authors are discussing at the time you commence your dissertation. Do not use dated material here, unless it is to show a timeline of how thinking in and around the subject has evolved over time. However, bear in mind that there will be a section in the proposal dedicated to the literature review.

Rationale

This is a relatively easy task to accomplish. It comprises of no more than a paragraph, which outlines the following:

- The reason(s) for the study;

- The new knowledge the study will bring to the table (now, do not worry about this; new knowledge can also mean knowledge that builds upon and adds to the existing knowledge);

- The motivation for the study; that is, why *you* have chosen the topic, and what it is that motivates *you* about the subject;

- Finally, who is likely to want to read the results of your research?

Defining the research question

This will largely be dependent on the issues you have highlighted in your background and rationale sections of your proposal. Therefore, '...you should be able to identify the particular part of the subject that you wish to investigate' (Walliman, 2005: p.72). It is crucial that you recognise that any subject you choose to study could in fact be researched for a number of years, or even a lifetime. Subsequently, you need to isolate one key area of the subject that you can manage; especially given the length of time you have in which to undertake your study. But it should still be able to take you out of your comfort zone in order to stretch you and give you the opportunity to evidence your new-found knowledge and skills that you have gained from undertaking a piece of unique research. Yes! Unique, because even if a fellow student undertakes a similar study to yours, it will still be completely different, as they are not you. Therefore, they may have a very different way of approaching the study, and observe things differently to the way you do, so do not allow yourself to be upset or stressed if you learn that another student is undertaking research on a similar subject area.

However, a word of caution needs to be given here. Do not be tempted to share your work with a fellow student, as you may find that software programs like TurnitinUK™ (a national database of all theses and assignments submitted at any university or college in the United Kingdom) and other similar checking software may find a match, and your supervisor may then suspect collusion or copying. Do not be tempted. This is *your* chance to shine and show what *you* have learned; do not let this unique opportunity pass you by.

Aim and objectives

The aim will provide a succinct summary of the study, which should be general and all encompassing (Bordens and Abbott, 2005; Quinlan, 2011).

The research objectives must have a measurable outcome. They allow you to break your research down into questions you want to ask of your target population. You can then turn these questions/areas of study into '**action**' statements, and ensure that they achieve a specific '**outcome**'. When setting objectives, they need to be set out as bullet points, and should consist of no more than **five** (you can go to six, if needed) bullet points (this is a norm in the UK, but may be different in other countries), but there must be no less than **four** bullet points. Good words to use when setting measurable objectives are:

36

- To identify...
- To determine...
- To create...
- To establish...
- To illustrate...
- To analyse... (Jackson, 2009)

Literature review

This is the foundation of any research undertaking and where you will identify the key areas you wish to study (see section on background). Undertaking a literature review allows you to narrow down your chosen subject area, and identifies any areas for further study and, of course, current thinking on the subject.

The literature review is where you will compare and contrast different key authors' views on the subjects/concepts/theories under discussion and relevant to your study, before applying them to your research question. However, you will not be able to undertake this fully in the proposal due to the limit placed on the word count. Nevertheless, you should still be able to give enough of a flavour of the different views on the subject(s) you are discussing and, just as important, of your ability to write academically. Do not worry about this too much, as you will make initial errors until you progress further with your studies. Nevertheless, this important exercise allows your supervisor to gauge where you are at, in terms of academic writing and analysis skills. He or she will guide you on how to improve your academic writing, and it may be prudent to see your institution's academic skills tutor(s). This will not just benefit you for your proposal and dissertation, but also for any other written pieces of work you may have to submit. The work you produce here can be used in the main dissertation but obviously it will need to be expanded upon and self-referenced to avoid self-plagiarising. This means you reference both yourself and your proposal in the dissertation.

As with any academic pieces of work, one should always provide an introduction; you should do this for each chapter in the main dissertation. However, for the proposal, I would suggest that you write an introduction for the literature review section; this will give an indication of the subject areas to be covered in the main dissertation and will highlight your understanding of what a literature review is. Furthermore, you should then select one of these subject areas you have indicated you will be reading around to formulate your discussion for the proposal. You will need to be reading widely, and it is highly recommended that you use journal articles to formulate your discussions, as they tend to be both current and/or contemporary. Avoid the use of Wikipedia as both academics and some (but not necessarily all) universities frown upon this.

Methodology

The methodology is similar to a system or procedure, in that it is a blueprint (plan) or framework describing how you propose to go about collecting your data. This sounds a relatively simple task to undertake; however, it is (from my experience) one of the main areas where many students lose valuable marks. The methodology should be approached with the same rigour as the literature review, as it can be viewed, in essence, like a literature review of research design, where you use key authors to support your discussions and to help justify the reasons for one adopted approach over another.

There is a point I wish to offer some clarification on here, and is often both confusing and misleading to students. Many texts refer to research philosophies as those of epistemology, ontology, and axiology. These are, indeed, the underpinning research philosophies. However, some authors then go on to refer to research philosophies as positivism, pragmatism, phenomenology, interpretivism, feminism, realism, and con- structivism, to name but a few. It is true that these are discussed as philosophies in their own right; however, for the sake of clarity, I refer to them as paradigms.

Paradigms are a:

> ...set of beliefs, values, and assumptions that a community of researchers has in common regarding the nature and conduct of research. The beliefs include, but are not limited to, ontological beliefs, epistemological beliefs, axiological beliefs, aesthetic beliefs, and methodological beliefs. Johnson, Onwuebuzie, and Turner (2007: pp.129-130) cited in Freshwater and Cahill, 2013: p.4

I have learnt recently that a few lecturers at some institutions here in the UK are moving away from undergraduates needing to have knowledge of these philosophies and paradigms. I would disagree with this view. For example, if you go on to study a master's degree, and you need to use these philosophies but do not know them, you may feel let down or, worse, inadequate; more so if the other students on the course have a working knowledge of them. Only this week, a past international student of mine (Jane), who is from China, came to visit me to say hello and let me know how she was getting on. She told me she had just finished her master's degree in London, which was brilliant. Jane went on to tell me how some of the students in her class in London had asked her how she knew about philosophies and paradigms, when they did not. Her answer was 'Because I was taught them by Dr Denis Feather at the University of Huddersfield.' Apparently these other students had not being given any insight into these philosophies and paradigms at their respective institutions. However, you, the reader, must decide whether to learn about the research philosophies and paradigms, and whether or not to include these in your methodology, as you have to submit work in line with your institution's guidelines. I would always advise my students to evidence that they have a basic understanding of these philosophies and paradigms, especially at undergraduate level.

A key model that most students tend to use here is Saunders et al.'s (2009) research onion. It will help keep you focused on what you have to incorporate within your methodology, but can be a little confusing; for example, when the outer ring is labelled 'philosophies', when instead it may have been better labelled 'research paradigms'. A possible alternative is the research methodology chain I have developed (see Figure 5.1 in Chapter 5), which offers a different perspective to that of the research onion. The following areas should be included in the methodology chapter.

Introduction

You should provide one or two sentences that provide a definition of what a research methodology is; that is, a blue print, plan, or set of instructions on how you approached your research and the methods you employed to capture your data.

Philosophies
When commencing your research, you will need to have a basic understanding of which philosophy or 'world view' your research is likely to fall under. At undergraduate level, there is not much emphasis on this, but it is useful if you have a basic understanding These research philosophies are epistemology, ontology, and axiology, and the paradigms fit under one or more of these.

Paradigms
This is where you will choose one or more of the paradigms (discussed earlier), for example interpretivism and positivism, and discuss why you have chosen these. You should highlight the advantages and disadvantages of the paradigm(s) adopted and why you have selected them. You will need to evidence that you have gained a good understanding of these, so again, reading around different authors' views on these is imperative.

The quantitative v. qualitative debate

There are two schools of thought on research design: one is the quantitative school and the other is the qualitative school (Clark, 1998). Some researchers believe that you should adopt either one research approach or the other, and there are those that vehemently argue that only quantitative approaches are viable, as qualitative research is too subjective. However, you need not worry too much about this at undergraduate level, *but you do need to be aware of it*, as your supervisor may fall into one of these schools of thought. It may be prudent to ascertain which school your supervisor prefers (if any) and then for you to discuss with them why you wish to adopt a particular approach. You need to remember that this is your project not your supervisor's (unless you are undertaking research for them), therefore you need to be polite but firm when you wish to take a particular approach. If your supervisor believes it is not the right approach, listen to what they have to say as to why, do some reading around the subject and then make your decision.

Mixed-method research

Today, there is much debate around using a mixed-method approach (Teddlie and Tashakkori, 2009); you can use a quantitative method with a qualitative method of data collection. For example, you could use a structured question-naire and a semi-structured interview schedule. You can also use a mixed-paradigm approach, where you might use positivism with interpretivism; some authors refer to this as triangulation; however, triangulation usually denotes the use of three approaches (hence 'tri' meaning three). Either way, you will need to read around the different philosophies and paradigms to see which are the best one(s) for your research, and then decide which to employ. You will need to make it explicitly clear to the reader as to why you have elected to use

41

this approach, and the advantages and disadvantages of using those selected.

Next we will consider the design of the research and its practicalities.

Sampling

You need to show your intended sample size – 100 is the norm for the use of quantitative questionnaires/surveys in a piece of undergraduate research. In addition, you need to include whether you are using non-probability sampling or probability sampling, and the number of interviews/focus groups you may be planning to use. You may need to agree the number of interviews needed with your supervisor, but between six and ten is usually acceptable for this level of study (Robson, 2002).

Questionnaire design/structure

You need to decide here whether the questionnaire is going to be structured, semi-structured, or unstructured? A structured questionnaire comprises of closed-ended questions, Likert scales and opinion questions. A semi-structured questionnaire is like a structured questionnaire but contains a small number of open-ended questions. An unstructured questionnaire contains only open-ended questions. You will need to indicate the types of questions that you are going to use, for example Likert scales, opinion questions, closed questions, or open-ended questions. Oppenheim (2001) wrote a book on questionnaire and interview design, and it is recommended that you consider its use when designing your own research questionnaire. Remember, aesthetics are just as important as the questions you intend to ask. The questions should be worded so that they are not leading or confusing, and must enable you to collect data to answer both your research question/hypotheses, and your research objectives.

Postal, electronic, or face-to-face: There are a number of ways to get your questionnaire in front of your target sample. For example, you could send it through the post, which was the norm at one time, but the response rate was around 14%. Whereby, if you need 100 fully completed questionnaires, you can quickly do the maths, and see that you would need to send out 1,400 questionnaires. "Well that's it" I can hear you saying to yourself. Do not give in so easily; what are you like? It is only a guide; no one has a crystal ball that can tell you how many you are likely to have returned completed; technology has helped the researcher a great deal in this area. Today, with the technological advances, more and more students are using online questionnaires, and then send these through their social networks such as Facebook™, LinkedIn™, or Twitter™. Face-to-face questionnaires are where you may stand outside a shop or organisation (after obtaining permission to do so) and ask the people that you stop if they would like to take part in your survey. You then ask the questions, and tick the relevant boxes for their answers. You will need to decide which is the best fit with your research.

Piloting: You will need to pilot the questionnaire in order to ensure that it is collecting the data necessary to answer the set research objectives for the study. Walliman (2005; p.168) writes, 'If you can, test it on people of a type similar to that of the intended sample to anticipate any problems of comprehension, or other sources of confusion.' This may identify to you any problems that may occur, for example if a question is not understood, or the instructions are not clear. Watch the body language of those respondents when piloting the questionnaire. If they knot their eyebrows, it is a clear indication that they do not understand something, or are not sure how to answer the question. (If the pilot questionnaire has gone via the post, you will not be able to do this, so gaining as much written feedback as possible is a necessity.) Ask them what it is about the questionnaire or a particular question that is making them pause for thought. In addition to this, ask the respondent to provide feedback on how they believe the questionnaire might be improved. As a result, you will need to build time into your research to pilot the questionnaire; the norm for undergraduate students is usually around ten piloted questionnaires to the target audience.

Pre-coding/post-coding: This is where you will pre-code the data for entry into SPSS – the Statistical Package for the Social Sciences (Robson, 2002: p.392), which is now known as 'Predictive Analytics SoftWare' or PASW. An alternative to PASW is Microsoft Excel, but your decision on which one to use will largely be dependent on your skills of using one or the other. However, data analysis is a highly sought-after skill in the commercial sector. I would recommend that you get yourself some training on PASW, as this will give you a new skill set on your curriculum vitae. See Figure 5.4 in Chapter 5 for examples of how pre-coded questions are formatted. Pre-coding can be undertaken on questions that are closed, opinion, or scaling in nature. However, with open-ended questions you will have to wait for the data to come back before you can start coding it. You will need to look for similarities in the answers provided, give them a category, and then post-code them. For example, suppose one of your questions asks the respondent to indicate their official job title. You then start to compile the different categories, i.e. manager, account manager, account handler, marketing assistant, and so on, and then post-code them similar to the pre-coding method above. You may find that account manager and account handler are the same job but identified differently at different institutions. As such, you would list these two together and identify you have done this in the results/findings chapter of your dissertation by giving it a designated heading and prescribing a code for analysis.

Interview schedule design

These tend to be viewed as qualitative research because you are endeavouring to gain people's views/perceptions/opinions on the subjects you raise for discussion in order to answer all or part of your research objectives (Denzin, 2003). You will need to design an interview schedule, which is for your use and not the participant's use. It is a kind of aide-mémoire (Robson, 2002). One way to do this is to set it out in a table (see Table 3.1).

In this section, you would place the script that you would read to the participant. It will lay out the reason for the research, why it is being undertaken, and the ethics employed, e.g. seeking permission (informed consent) to tape record the interview. Also about the participant's rights to anonymity, etc.	
Q1. Just to get the interview started, how long have you been in marketing?	If answers just one or two years, ask them to elaborate on what they have done.
Q2. What do you think of the comments saying that advertising is dead?	If gives just one answer, probe participant further. Ask him/her to elaborate on interesting points raised.
Q3.	
Q4.	

Table 3.1 Example of an interview schedule (Feather, 2009).

As you can see from the table, you may have your questions in the left-hand column, and in the right-hand column you may have comments to remind you to probe for a deeper under-standing of what has been said, by asking the participant to elaborate on interesting points that they raise. You can also use the right-hand column to make notes on points raised that you may wish to revisit once the participant has finished talking; this way you do not disrupt their or your train of thought and the flow of the interview.

There are many data collection techniques, and you can find these in any good research design books. Universities also tend to have very good websites that aid students to understand the different research methods and tools available to researchers; for example, at my institution, information can be found at http://onlineqda.hud.ac.uk/ Remember, you will need to justify why you have adopted one technique over another, and the advantages and disadvantages of the different techniques to be used.

Data analysis (quantitative)

In this section, you will need to establish which software package or analytical technique you are going to employ. For example, you may decide to use PASW (SPSS) or Excel to analyse your quantitative data. Most students opt for PASW because it reproduces the calculations in tablature format, which is the advantage over Excel as this software only shows the graphs, but not necessarily the calculations. You will also need to identify what types of calculations you intend to use when testing different variables.

Data analysis (qualitative)

There is also software available for the analysis of qualitative data, known as NU:DIST – Non-numerical, Unstructured Data Indexing, Searching and Theorizing (Robson, 2002: p.456). It allows you to look for similarities in the transcripts you have entered into the program, and then produces different data to either support or formulate your discussions in the 'findings and analysis' section of your main dissertation. However, today, 'NVivo' is the software package that many qualitative researchers use to analyse the narratives they have collected from their interviewees. It is not easy software to use, but with some patience, training, and practice it can be mastered. Nevertheless, this will largely be dependent on the time you have to do this, which may be limited to say the least. You might elect to adopt one of the more traditional methods, of 'content analysis', or 'thematic analysis'. See Silverman (2002) for a better understanding of the different qualitative data methods and analyses that can be employed.

Reliability and validity

You need a short statement here about the reliability and validity of your research. Walliman (2005: p.133) writes, 'It is…a rash researcher who insists on the infallibility of his or her data, and of the findings derived from them.'

Data can be misleading because it is elusive and ephemeral (Walliman, 2005). You are capturing data at a particular moment – somewhat akin to taking a photograph – and therefore if you asked the same people the same questions in a day, a month or in a year's time, it is highly likely that you would acquire data different to that collected earlier. This is because people, their environments, and other factors change. Another factor to consider is the participant's state of mind. For example, you may have interviewed a person on a particular day when, a few hours previously, they had been praised for doing a good job and received a promotion. A month later, you may go back and interview the same person, and find that the answers you are receiving are out of kilter with the ones you gained earlier; what you may not have been aware of prior to your interview is that they had just been made redundant. Therefore, you are going to obtain data from a person in different mind-sets, one positive, and the other negative.

Concerning validity, Walliman (2005: p.123) writes, 'The validity of deductive arguments is determined only by their logical form, not by the content of the statements which they contain.' He goes onto say:

> When the premise or premises of such an argument are related
> to the conclusion in such a way that the conclusion must be true
> if the premises are true, then the argument is said to be 'valid'.
> Any argument where this is not the case is called invalid.
> (Walliman, 2005: p.123)

Bias

Again you should have a short statement on how you are going to
manage this and the different types of bias that may influence
your research. For example, imagine you are stood in a shopping
precinct, and you have stated in your sample section of the
methodology that you are going to use your questionnaire on
every fifth person that passes you. You finish your interview and
are now looking for the next. Four people walk past, and you look
at the fifth person walking towards you. You observe that he is a
big burley man, with long hair, tattoos all the way up his arms,
and has metal chains hanging from his nose to his ear. He looks
like he has not had a wash in weeks, and he is talking to himself.
During this quick summarisation, you immediately decide to let
this person walk past, and you look to the floor so that you do not
make eye contact with him; the man passes you by. You have just
practised what is called 'selective bias' (Torgerson and Torgerson,
2003). If you read their paper and others on research bias, you will
get an indication of how to reduce research bias. One way is to
ensure you are objective. When interviewing, for example, ask
your interviewees the same questions, verbatim, as you have
them written down. Additionally, you should not ask leading
questions. The internal validity of your research, as well as the
external validity of research, is important to reducing bias.
Validity is discussed later in the book.

Limitations

In this section, you should identify the limitations you foresee
having a possible impact upon your research; for example,

sampling identification, or access to the people you need to interview. Time limitations could be another factor. Remember you will have other assignments to undertake whilst you are trying to conduct your research; you may even be holding down a full- or part-time job. Resources also need to be considered as your research is self-funded: you will have to produce questionnaires, and maybe print them off and post them.

Ethical considerations

All research will have some ethical considerations; for example, participant anonymity. The person taking part in the interview or completing the questionnaire has rights and these must be upheld. If you are considering interviewing children, this could be problematical; there are CRB (Criminal Records Bureau) checks (in the UK) to consider and these are costly. Alternatively, you would have to contact the parents to gain parental consent or the head teacher of the school, but again, this can be time-consuming and not without some cost, and therefore probably best avoided. However, this is where your supervisor will be of help as she or he will be able to offer alternative solutions and guide you in the right direction. You may also need to reflect upon possible moral dilemmas, or health and safety issues in regard to both yourself and that of your participants. A good start, concerning research ethics, is to check out the policies set by professional bodies, such as the following:

- British Educational Research Association (BERA) at www.bera.ac.uk/publications/guides.php

- American Educational Research Association (AERA) at http://www.aera.net/

- Market Research Society at www.mrs.org.uk/code.htm

Also, check your own institution's Intranet, as their research sites may contain guidelines on conducting ethical research and its practice.

Timeframe

In this section, you will identify when you are going to start and finish the different tasks needed to complete the study. A simple way to do this is via a Gantt chart, (see Figure 5.3 in Chapter 5).

Bibliography

This is an area where students tend to fall down, largely due to copying and pasting references into their bibliography. As such, these copied references do not always keep their format, nor are they always in the Harvard format. There are, today, various bibliographic software packages such as Endnote™, which can be an invaluable time-saver. For example, Endnote has a tool called 'cite while you write', which builds the bibliography up for you as you go along. In fact, I have used this package to produce the bibliography for this book, and the large number of papers I have published in journals.

A bibliography **should not** be separated into sections that list journal articles, books, websites, etc. The bibliography should run in an alphabetical format, irrespective of whether it is a book, journal article, or website.

Appendices

These are the last pages to appear in the thesis. A major mistake many students make is to place a number of images or tables on one page. An appendix should carry only one image or one table per page. Otherwise, it could become confusing when you are referring the reader to these in your discussions.

Additionally, many institutions do not count the appendices in the word count; but **do not** use this to get around the set number of words for the assessment. Only material that would disrupt the flow of the discussion should appear in the appendices.

Assessment

This will be largely down to your own institution's policies and procedures for the submitting and assessment of proposals and dissertations. Ensure that you are fully familiar with the format and deadlines for submitting.

In many institutions, it is the norm to submit two hardbound copies. Again, the type of binding will be particular to each institution – some institutions still like the theses to be bound in 'black buckram', whilst others will accept spiral binding, or even electronic copies. This information will be specific to your institution and they will provide you with the information you need.

It is now almost universally true to say that the electronic copy of your dissertation will be uploaded to TurnitinUK™ or other similar software as part of the university's plagiarism checking process. This will also allow your supervisor to check on your adherence to the set word limit for the proposal.

Assessment criteria that may be looked for in a dissertation proposal may look something like the following, which are taken from a UK university:

First-class grade:
In addition to the criteria set for upper second-class grade, there also must be:
Evidence of extensive reading and use of literature to substantiate arguments;
Critical evaluation;

Depth of insight;
Originality in exposition.

Upper second-class grade:

Evidence of wide reading;

Quality and depth of analysis to support sections in the proposal;

Demonstration of critical evaluation;

Evidence of good linking of objectives, literature review and methodology;

Justification of research practicalities adopted, along with advantages and disadvantages of each practicality;

A well presented report.

Lower second-class grade:

Evidence of a report that indicates NO collusion or collaboration with others in the writing stage;

Evidence of understanding the research methods and the research practicalities;

Clearly articulated;

There may be some evidence of the advantages and disadvantages of one or two research practicalities;

Demonstrates that the research proposal is relatively sound, and contains a clear description of what the student intends to do;

Report is clear and well written;

Some referencing will have been attempted.

Third-class grade:

Proposal is sparse with little or no evidence of wider reading;

Research practicalities are not fully addressed;

No discussion provided around the quantitative or qualitative approaches;

Little understanding is demonstrated;

Arguments are not substantiated; few or no references;
Poor presentation of report, large number of typing errors, and spelling mistakes;
Insufficient information to reproduce the study.

Fail:
Report is sparse, no evidence of reading or understanding of research methods and subject under discussion;
Numerous errors, omissions, or irrelevances;
No evidence of comparing or contrasting of key authors' views in the literature review and in the methodology.

Plagiarism

This is an important point **you must** consider. The researcher (you) must reference any author's idea or work you use within your own thesis, including your own work that you take from past assignments, or even from the proposal for your dissertation. Your work *must* be your own, and be original; it must not be plagiarised (Jankowicz, 2007; Gray, 2009). Plagiarism is:

> ...copying from someone else's work...Very occasionally, tutors encounter deliberate plagiarism, where an entire project report [or thesis], or a significant section, is taken from another person's work. If they [the tutors] can prove it, the consequences are ruinous and terminal for the student concerned. (Jankowicz, 2007: p.56)

In other words, if plagiarism is proven, then you will fail the dissertation module; you may fail your entire degree course; you may even be expelled from the university –

SO DON'T DO IT!

In reality, there is more to plagiarism than just copying, therefore ensure that you totally familiarise yourself with your institution's format for referencing (Gray, 2009) and their policies on what they consider to be plagiarism.

A recent trend that has become apparent since I wrote the first edition of this book is that of 'secondary referencing'. It never ceases to amaze me the amount of effort some students will expend to try to beat the system, rather than focusing that energy on the task.

'Secondary referencing' is where a student reads a textbook or an article, and will then claim that the reference is one they have looked at and used. For example, let us take my passage above where I have used Gray (2009) as a reference.

The student has read my book, and has written the following:

> 'When considering plagiarism, there is more to this than first meets the eye, and as such, one needs to familiarise themselves with their institution's format for referencing.'

Ok, nothing wrong so far, but when referencing to support this extract, instead of using '(Gray, 2009 cited by Feather, 2013, p. 26)' to reference correctly, they [the student] instead reference the work as if they had taken it from Gray themselves, but in reality have never looked at Gray's work. Therefore, the passage from the student would read:

> 'When considering plagiarism, there is more to this than first meets the eye, and as such, one needs to familiarise themselves with their institution's format for referencing (Gray, 2009).'

Without matching software packages such as TurnitinUK™, one would not necessarily pick this up as a paragraph that is plagiarised.

Today, many institutions are using software to identify and alert the tutor(s) to the possibility of plagiarism (Gray, 2009) within a submitted piece of work. Make sure this does not happen to you. Discuss your referencing with your supervisor, submit regular drafts so they can see how you are using referencing within your work, and make use of the learning development group/ academic skills tutors. They are there to help you.

Your 30-second recap

Your proposal is an important document that provides an indication of the level you're currently researching at, and the standard of writing you're producing.

Remember the different elements you need to cover in the research proposal.

Plagiarism is taken very seriously; you mustn't fall into its grasp.

Note the marking criteria you need to benchmark against.

Chapter 4: Okay, the proposal has been accepted, so what's next?

Introduction

Here is where the real reading starts, and your journey of knowledge acquisition begins. When commencing any research journey, everything starts and ends with reviewing relevant literature. Notice I use the term 'relevant'; this is an important term as it is very easy to fall into what I call 'reader's drift'. Reader's drift is where you are reading and making notes on one set of information, and before you know it, you are reading and making notes on other information that is not relevant to your study.

You need to use this chapter in combination with Chapter 3 as you will have produced a small overview of literature for the proposal.

It will be through reading around your chosen idea that you will identify any holes in the literature that need plugging, or where it is possible to extend existing knowledge (Robson, 2002). Additionally, the reviewing of relevant literature will continue right up until you are ready to write the final draft of your thesis; this way you remain current in your subject area. It is also a way of evidencing to your supervisor and external examiners that you have read widely on the subject. It is here that your research journal note-taking and the accuracy of those notes will prove crucial to your research, as is the proper recording of citations and the correct use of referencing. Revisit

Chapter 2 and the websites mentioned there to reinforce your knowledge and understanding of this.

Where do I start?

This is a question I am often asked by my students, and it is not easy to put into words, but there are some simple questions you should ask yourself that may help with this question. These are:

1. What exactly do I need to cover in my literature review?

2. What are the theories and concepts that need to be included?

3. How do I apply these concepts and theories to my particular study?

4. What are the data resources I need access to? (Sekaran and Bougie, 2009)

Defining a literature review

There are numerous definitions on what constitutes a literature review, for example:

Ridley (2012: p.3) writes that:

> The 'literature review' is the part of the thesis where there is extensive reference to *related research and theory* [my emphasis] in your field; it is where connections are made between the source texts that you draw on and where you position yourself and your research among these sources.

Aveyard (2010: p.5) argues that a literature review is '...the comprehensive study and interpretation of literature that relates to a particular topic'.

From these two definitions, it can be seen that the similarities are that the literature review is both an extensive and comprehensive piece of work. However, Ridley (2012) extends this to discuss positioning; that is, where your review is grounded. You need to ensure that the concepts and theories that are part of your research, or where your research study is focusing, are grounded in this literature. This means not losing focus on what it is you are attempting to cover.

Creswell (2009: p.25) may agree with the above when writing that a literature review:

> ...accomplishes several purposes. It shares with the reader the results of other studies that are closely related to the one being undertaken. It relates a study to the larger, ongoing dialogue in the literature, filling in gaps and extending prior studies (Cooper, 198; Marshall & Rossman, 2006). It provides a framework for establishing the importance of the study as well as a benchmark for comparing the results with other findings.

However Maylor and Blackmon (2005: p.117) write that a literature review

> ...is a critical analysis of the...research on your topic that positions your research in its theoretical context, shows that you understand the current state of the research topic and supports any conceptual framework (theories, models, hypotheses) that you plan to investigate.

From these viewpoints, it can be seen that there are some further additions introduced when defining a literature review. For example, Creswell (2009) argues that it provides a framework, but then again, so does Maylor and Blackmon (2005). However, the former argues from the perspective that it establishes the importance of the study; the latter discusses the framework for theories, models, and hypotheses. Nevertheless, you need to be careful when discussing such terminology like those of 'conceptual frameworks'; this particular term relates to the whole process of the thesis, or what Quinlan (2011) refers to as the 'four framework approach'. The theoretical framework is, in reality, the literature review. Maylor and Blackmon (2005) do identify an important point however, which is that the review should be critical. Having said this, I have something I need to make you, the reader, aware of. When reflecting on the term 'conceptual framework', this in itself is a paradox. Why do I say this? Let's use phenomenology and strip it apart; let's be critical. When discussing a concept this is an idea, a thought, which is not reality, and is intangible. However, when discussing the term 'framework', it is a structure, a procedure to follow. Therefore, how can one have something that is so subjective, linked with something that is rigid, planned? Obviously, the two are not compatible. So think carefully when using terms such as these.

Being critical is an important skill that you will need to learn, and one that can only be undertaken when you have read enough texts to allow you to practise this. Your supervisor and the learning development group and/or the academic skills tutors at your institution should be able to help you develop this skill further. There are also some very good textbooks (that are easy to read) to help you develop your critiquing skills. For example, see the book by Wallace and Wray (2011) entitled *Critical Reading and Writing for Postgraduates*. Now, do not be put off by the use of the word 'postgraduate' in the title; the examples and exercises are very easy to follow and undertake, and it is my opinion that this book may help you develop these skills further.

Having discussed the above, it is evident that defining the term 'literature review' is complex, possibly bordering on the super complex (Hart, 2008). Hart (2008) discusses how the research approach is similar to that of an apprenticeship, where the apprentice learns via observation, reading, and practice. Putting this in context, your supervisor may have some papers they have written or excellent examples of past theses, which you could look at in order to get a feel of how to structure the review. There are volumes of books on research methods (Cohen et al., 2000; de Vaus, 2003; Easterby-Smith et al., 2004; Hart, 2008), and more specifically on how to under-take a literature review, that you can read in order to obtain a deeper understanding of what is needed to make your review stand out from others.

One of the hardest things for any writer is to start writing; that blank screen with the flashing cursor almost dares you to type something, or the blank sheet of paper with your pen poised, but no words will come. Do not worry; this is a common feeling amongst most researchers, even those that are accomplished at this practice. Writing does not comes easy for most people, but the skill is to write little and often. The main thing is to start writing; write anything. Once you start, you will be surprised how quickly you get into it. I can hear you saying, 'That is ok for you to say, you are an academic and have written both articles and books'. Believe me when I tell you, I have laboured hard on every single one of them. Yes, I may have a better understanding than some, but it does not make the task any easier. The number of times I have written something in this revised edition, and then started over, because I did not think anyone would understand what I was talking about. Furthermore, whilst copy-editing, I've considered different ways of communicating information to you to help you understand and apply it to your learning.

I have read numerous books on how to write well, on how to improve my grammar and punctuation, because I am dyslexic; some have helped, others have not. I have asked professors how to improve my writing, but was merely told to keep writing. Nevertheless, what if I keep writing, but not in the correct way for me and therefore I don't improve. Subsequently, if my writing does not improve, I am still stuck at 'square one'. What I have found useful is to listen to those that at least offer some advice that I can use, and then decide if it works for me. Another book that really helped me was *Critical Thinking for Psychology* by Forshaw (2012); you may find this of use. Finally, you need to practise, practise, practise, and then practise some more! Additionally, you need to seek formative feedback on your writing from those who you identify as good writers, academics, academic skills tutors/learning development group, professors, editors (if you know any), and so on.

Coming back to the literature review process, Hart (2008: p.13) defines a literature review as:

> The selection of available documents (both published and unpublished) on the topic, which contain information, ideas, data and evidence written from a particular standpoint to fulfil certain aims or express certain views on the nature of the topic and how it is to be investigated, and the effective evaluation of these documents in relation to the research being proposed.

This is, in fact, a reasonable working definition, which covers all the bases, and one that I have adopted for this guide.

Purpose of the literature review in research

By reading around your chosen subject area, you are making a commitment to yourself and your future reader that you have become very familiar with the current studies in your topic, and in the history of the topic; in other words, what has come before. This will allow you to make the connections between different authors' viewpoints and to offer critiques where possible (Bordens and Abbott, 2005; Hart, 2008). Hart (2008) identifies a number of purposes that the literature review will serve:

1. Distinguishing what has been done from what needs to be done;

2. Discovering important variables relevant to the topic;

3. Synthesising and gaining a new perspective;

4. Identifying relationships between ideas and practice;

5. Establishing the context of the topic or problem;

6. Rationalising the significance of the problem;

7. Enhancing and acquiring the subject vocabulary;

8. Understanding the structure of the subject;

9. Relating ideas and theory to applications;

10. Identifying the main methodologies and research techniques that have been used;

11. Placing the research in a historical context to show familiarity with state-of-the-art developments (Hart, 2008: p.27).

This is a good overview. As regards point 10, the methodologies the different authors use (that you read) may give you some indication of the types of philosophies and methods you may wish to use. For example, you may wish to reproduce the experiment the original author uses, or to spot flaws in their methods, which might allow you to uncover new knowledge.

Structure

The structure of the literature review is another important part of the process and one of the most likely places where you can gain or lose grades. I always say to my students, "Remember the 3 Ts."

*   Tell me what you are going to tell me. This is the introduction to the literature review. What are the concepts and theories you intend to cover and how do they relate to your study?

*   Tell me. This is the main discussion with headings and sub-headings. Ensure you cover all the concepts and theories you have identified and that you have related them to your research statement and/or question. Remember your discussion must 'fit' (Quinlan, 2011) with your research subject; do not forget how easy it is to succumb to reader's drift.

- Tell me what you have told me. This is the summary or conclusion of the section (proposal) or the chapter (dissertation). With the conclusion, it is slightly different in that here you pull out the key findings from your research. You cease being objective, and instead put forward an argument based on the key findings in relation to your research objectives, whereby you answer the set research question(s).

Look to the marking criteria for this section in your dissertation module booklet, as it will identify what is required by your institution in order to obtain a good grade. In addition, have regular meetings with your supervisor and ascertain if she or he is willing to look at drafts of your work. An important point to remember here is that the marking criteria for the literature review for the thesis may change from what is required for the proposal, so ensure you know exactly what is expected of you in both instances.

The 3 Cs

These are comparing, contrasting, and critiquing different authors' viewpoints on the concepts and theories you discuss, or indeed any other relevant text (see the recommended book earlier on critiquing). There are always two sides to an argument in academia: those for and those against the argument. I have evidenced one way of doing this above, in the section on defining a literature review. It is your role to be objective and show both sides of a discussion before formulating your own argument, which needs to be supported with credible references. If you do not support your arguments, the discussion may be merely viewed as conjecture and/or supposition, and as a result you may lose valuable marks.

I always advise my students to **reference every single sentence that carries a fact, figure, statement, or idea**. This sounds a bit over-the-top at first glance, but believe me when

I say that most of what you write will incorporate one or more of these points. In addition, by referencing, what you are saying to the reader is, "Hey, I have read this material, put it in my own words, and these people support what I have written. If you do not believe me, look to the reference in the bibliography and see for yourself." It is also a good way of evidencing to your supervisor and any other reader of your work that you have really read and understood the subject, concepts, theories or ideas, and can apply them; this is achieved when you apply the above approach to your study. In terms of applying, this is where you use real-life examples to which you apply the concepts, or when applying the concepts and theories to your research idea/topic.

A very dirty word

I am going to use a four-letter word now (although I have used it many times previously, but I need to really drive this point home). It may un-nerve some of you, and if it does, I apologise, as there is no other way of saying it. In order to undertake a literature review, you must **READ!** It is at this time in your studies when you need to be forward planning, to have your eye on the horizon concerning the grade you wish to have on your degree qualification, and the amount of work you have to undertake. Only you can do the reading, only you can do the work; it is not your supervisor's job to find material for you, or indeed write it for you. By this stage in your degree, you are supposed to be what is known as an 'autonomous learner', or what I have deemed to call a 'student practitioner'; that is, you know how to find things for yourself. The more reading (sorry, I said it again) you do, the more you become focused in on your subject, where eventually you will become the expert on that particular topic.

A Word of Warning! 🚫

Today, there are various people offering students a service (and I use this term very loosely), where for a fee they say they will write the student's dissertation for them, guaranteeing that the student will pass. Do not be fooled. One reason is that we as academics can spot in an instant a change of tone and style of writing from past works of the student to the one that has been produced fraudulently. Yes, I use the term 'fraudulently', because that is what it is. Do you want to go through life as a fraud? Second, it will (without any doubt) be spotted by the various software packages that we use in academia, and when you are found out, the penalty could be severe. These people promise you the world and deliver you an 'off-the-shelf' piece, which they have written for someone else. These people are unscrupulous. All I will say to you is *Caveat Emptor* – 'Buyer Beware'; you have been warned! You have invested a great deal of time and money in getting to where you are now; do not throw it all away because you think the task is too hard. Rise to the challenge and show your real metal.

Valuable tips

When you find an article that is relevant to your study, the first thing you should do is visit the references at the end, so you can see what references the author(s) have used in their work, and if there are any that are relevant to your study. A further tip is to look at the key words the author(s) use (especially in journal articles), as this will allow you to use the same key words when searching online.

Google Scholar is another good place to find resources. It will also identify who has cited that piece of work, and from there will give you a lead into other authors' works.

Referencing

You are probably fed-up with hearing about this, but it is extremely important, especially if you wish to avoid plagiarising, (referred to today as 'poor academic integrity'). Most institutions use the Harvard referencing format, but I will guarantee you that no two institutions will be the same. Certainly, those I have studied and worked at in my time have had different ways of interpreting the Harvard system. Your supervisor should help you with this, as should your academic skills tutors/learning development groups. However, most institutions' libraries carry some form of handout or online version that can help you with this.

Another trend that has developed since I wrote the first edition, and which I touched upon earlier, is that many universities appear to be moving towards the American Psychological Association (APA) 6th format of referencing. Your library should offer a guide on how to use this style; make sure you have it to hand. If anyone tells you it is the same as Harvard, they are telling you tales. There are unique differences, which you will have to learn and incorporate into your work.

One alternative to using a guide manual is the option to use a bibliographic software package, such as Endnote™ from Adept Science. There is a valuable tool (one of many) within Endnote called 'cite while you write', which produces your reference or bibliography for you as you insert the reference from the list of references you have entered into your personal library (its database). You even do not have to go this far if you do not want to because, with the marvel of new technology, you can download the reference straight into Endnote, thus ensuring that you capture all of the relevant data needed to reference correctly. Endnote has a whole plethora of different referencing styles. All you need to do is tick a box to say which one you are using (well, there is a little more to it than that, but in simple terms, that is all you are doing). There are other bibliographic software packages available; see which one you prefer, if you decide to use one.

A word of warning though. Many software tools such as Endnote may be platform-specific and will only work correctly when the file is read with the same software and operating system that created it. Obviously, this does not affect the printed copy, but your electronic copy submitted for similarity checking may be. A colleague recently had the experience of a correctly cited and referenced document using Endnote that had had all the citations and references stripped out when the file was read on another machine with different software. It would be wise to do a test run to ensure that the similarity checking software does not do this to you. If your institution has asked that you submit your work as a PDF file, it may be that you do not experience this problem, but many universities still have students submit their work as a Word document.

Summaries

It is good practice to summarise each of your main chapters, except the conclusions chapter, as this is itself a summary. If you summarise the key findings at the end of each chapter, it will make your life a little easier when it comes to writing up your conclusion and recommendations chapter. Why? Because you will have already done this at the end of each chapter and therefore will be mainly (as one of my students referred to it as) "sewing it all together".

Your 30-second recap

I've shown you how to reference using the Harvard format.

I've provided you with a working definition for the term 'literature review'.

Structure your discussions better by using the 3T model of 'Tell me what you are going to tell me, tell me, and tell me what you have told me'.

I've also introduced you to the 3C model of 'compare, contrast, and critique'; these three tenets are the three cornerstones of any reviewing process you undertake.

To undertake a good literature review you'll need to have the required depth of knowledge in order to accomplish this.

Reading (sorry, I just can't help myself!) is the only way you're going to obtain knowledge.

You need to work hard at getting tacit knowledge for yourself.

Identify a time and place where you work at your optimum.

Keep this time sacrosanct and let everyone know that you are serious when you're working on your dissertation.

Apply the above process to every concept/theory/subject you discuss, weaving the whole chapter into a coherent whole.

Chapter 5: I know what I want to research, but I don't know how

Introduction to research methodology

The marking criteria for the dissertation are likely to carry different weightings for the grading of this chapter in your dissertation thesis to that of your research proposal. See the module booklet that your institution provides for this information. For example, at the institution I work for, there is more weighting given to the methodology in the proposal than in the main dissertation. The reasoning behind this is that if you can get it right for the proposal, it should be a straightforward process of transferring this knowledge to the research methodology chapter in the thesis; however, remember to self-reference. It is also because in the thesis there is more weighting given to the analysis chapter; and in the methodology chapter you may be just making a few corrections or alterations, depending upon what has influenced your research whilst you were undertaking the primary data collection, and writing up the various chapters of your thesis. Therefore, you may be in a position where you are simply tightening up your writing in line with your supervisor's comments, using the feedback you received on this section in your proposal, and changing the present tense to the past tense.

Having said this, in all my years of experience supervising and grading students' work, this chapter appears to be the weak link in the chain of writing for the undergraduate dissertation. This is mainly because it may be the first time that students have been introduced to such concepts as phenomenology, inter-pretivism, epistemology, feminism, action research, positivism, and so on. These are very scary words to some students (Quinlan, 2011). Nevertheless, they should not put you off, as it is these words, and the knowledge acquired by reading, understanding, and applying these words, that will make your work stand out from other students' work. Further, it may allow you to gain those extra marks you feel you may need in order to meet your desired objective of obtaining a good grade for your dissertation, and therefore counting towards your final degree classification. Therefore, it is important that you get this part right: it is your plan of action that you will undertake (present tense and future tense for the proposal) or have undertaken (past tense for the dissertation) for your chosen research subject.

Where to start

The hardest aspect of academic work, or for any period of writing, is where to start. There are numerous books that you can read on how to conduct your research (Robson, 2002; Booth and Harrington, 2003; de Vaus, 2003; Easterby-Smith et al., 2004; Bordens and Abbott, 2005; Maylor and Blackmon, 2005; Gray, 2009; Saunders et al., 2009; Teddlie and Tashakkori, 2009; Quinlan, 2011; Garner, 2012), but the hardest task is actually starting to write.

What I do when faced with this situation is to just start writing, putting my thoughts down on paper. I usually end up throwing some of the work away, but at least I have started, and this is what I advise you to do. You can bring it all together when you know exactly what you are doing, and have had the opportunity to chat with your supervisor. However, when it comes to this particular chapter, you will need to get yourself a couple of good reference books and start there. One of the books I tend to advise

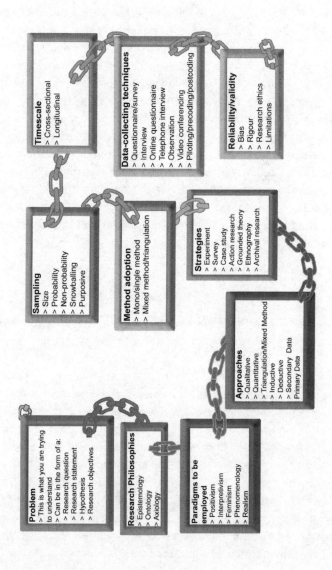

Figure 5.1 The research methodology chain.

my students to get hold of is *Research Methods for Business Students* by Saunders et al. (2007). On page 132 of the book, the authors have designed a research onion; it is an adaptation of Husserl's 'Onion for Phenomenology' (Moran and Mooney, 2002) and works quite well as an aide-mémoire. However, I need to express a point of view here: there are some aspects of this model that can be confusing to some students, and in some places may be flawed or misleading. As a result, I have produced a research methodology chain model (Figure 5.1) that may be easier to follow and of more use. I have adapted this from Saunders et al.'s (2007: p.207) research onion. It could also be used as a checklist for you to ensure that you have the necessary elements needed in your methodology. Let me explore these different elements in a little more detail.

Re-stating the research question

It is well worth restating here the problem, research question, and/or hypothesis of your research, as this may not have been covered since the first part of your proposal and the first chapter in your thesis. It is also wise to reiterate what your objectives are. This is good practice, and will reinforce to both you and your reader what it is you are intending to measure and how they *fit* with your research statement/question (Quinlan, 2011). Remember, that your objectives should be both specific and measurable (think SMART), and should comprise of no less than four bullet points, but no more than six bullet points (revisit Chapter 3 on writing aims and objectives). One point you *will* need to remember is that you should evidence the advantages and disadvantages for each approach/strategy you have chosen to adopt throughout your methodology.

Philosophies

Here we get to the scary bit. This is where many undergraduate students tend to switch off, because the words they encounter scare them (Quinlan, 2011). In fact, this is where undergraduate students should be **switching on**, as it is something completely new that they may be learning, and is useful both in business/ marketing research and in academic research. Remember, at undergraduate level you do not need to be a master in these different philosophies, but a basic understanding will help you appreciate how all the pieces of the jigsaw fit together. Many students miss these philosophies out and tend to approach this aspect of the methodology by stating that their research will simply be either qualitative or quantitative in nature. The better students will realise that the use of both approaches aids in offering rigour to their research (Robson, 2002; Saunders et al., 2007). However, the crunch comes when your supervisor asks you which qualitative or quantitative approach you have adopted for your research. Therefore, you need to have a good working knowledge of the philosophies you intend to adopt. In the methodology, you need to make it crystal clear to the reader which philosophy(ies) you are adopting, and why. In other words, how your jigsaw pieces fit together.

Remember, the research philosophies are epistemology, ontology, and axiology; I have listed them so that you are aware of them. In other words, I am planting the seed of knowledge in you, with the view that it might take hold and grow. These are more prevalent for master's and doctoral students, but there is no reason why you should not use them if you wish. In fact, if you do plan to continue with your studies, it is probably a good thing; it will certainly broaden your viewpoint. However, if you get confused by these do not worry; at undergraduate level, you really do not need to have a fine grasp of what they are about, and how they are used. But, as I said, they do underpin everything we as researchers practice.

Positivism, interpretivism, phenomenology, feminism, critical realism, pragmatism and so on when used in research methodology become paradigms (although they are philosophies in their own right). They fit under epistemology, ontology, and axiology. As a result, together, they offer a homogeneous approach to designing research.

Having said this, this is where those books I spoke of earlier will really come into good use. This, however, may raise a problem; you may be part of a large cohort of students, probably all searching frantically for the same books. Just because you are, for example, business students, does not mean that you cannot look at education books or psychology books on research design – the philosophies and paradigms are a constant no matter which subject you are studying. Moreover, it may work in your favour as you may obtain a different perspective, and will be seen by your supervisor as being more widely read.

This brings me onto a further problem. Many students read books and journals, but if these texts say the same sort of things, students will discard the other books and journals and instead only reference one. The secret is to use them all. For example, interpretivism is looking at how people interpret their world and make sense of it (Cohen et al., 2000; Williams, 2000; Robson, 2002; Saunders et al., 2007). The other important aspect is that students tend not to offer the same diligence to this chapter as they may to their literature review or, indeed, other chapters. However, as I have already said, the methodology chapter for many students appears to be the weak link in the dissertation chain.

Having said this, you can elect to undertake a triangulation/ mixed philosophical approach to your research. This is where you may use a number of paradigms to offer more of an academic rigour to your research, thus offering more reliability and validity to your findings. For example, you may elect to use the interpretivist paradigm with a realist paradigm, thereby offering both a qualitative and quantitative approach to your research. In other words, by comparing what is 'understood' by those who interpret their world with that which is 'understood' by those who believe what is there is what exists.

Approaches

When designing your research methodology, there are two approaches that you can adopt for your study; one is the 'deductive' approach, and the second is the 'inductive' approach.

Deductive

Here you become a detective, somewhat like Sherlock Holmes, looking purely at data (facts and figures) from a scientific perspective. Subsequently, you may come up with an idea(s) or build on an existing idea(s) from your readings; you may or may not test a hypothesis – this will be largely dependent on whether you are undertaking a qualitative or quantitative piece of research (Cohen et al., 2000; Saunders et al., 2007).

Observation was introduced to the deductive approach by Francis Bacon in the 1600s as he felt that deductive reasoning was not robust enough (Cohen et al., 2000). As Saunders et al. (2007: p.57) writes:

> For some research projects, you will use the literature to help you identify theories and ideas that you will test using data. This is known as a **deductive approach** [emphasis in original], in which you develop a theoretical or conceptual framework, which you subsequently test, using data.

The testing of your hypothesis/theory via the use of statistical data is where you will either confirm or refute (reject) your hypothesis/theory.

Inductive

The inductive approach is where you undertake your research based around observations or an idea, and let the theory come out at the end of your research. On this, Saunders et al. (2007: p. 57) writes that: 'For other research projects you will be planning to explore your data and to develop theories from them that you will subsequently relate to the literature.' This does not mean that you will not have a research question, aim, or measurable objectives: you will, as you will still need a well-defined purpose to the research. It means that you will not start with a conceptual framework or a predetermined theory (Saunders et al., 2007), but it will be expected that you are well versed in the subject area that you have chosen because you have read sufficiently widely to formulate a workable idea to research (see Quinlan, 2011: on how to develop a research question). For example, your research theory could be built around the question, or tentative hypothesis of: 'Is direct marketing dead?' Here you will commence your reading, and put together a viewpoint from which to develop questions to put to people you have identified as key to your research in order to gather their opinions and ideas. Afterwards, you will compare their answers with the secondary research you have already undertaken. Then you can put forward a possible theory or solution to the tentative hypothesis you may have developed on whether direct marketing is or is not dead.

Secondary data

This is all the data you have access to; for example, reports, journals, books, textbooks, trade magazines, company websites, and many more. The key point to remember here is that they have to be credible resources, as you wish for your research to offer good academic rigour. As such, as I have said before, Wikipedia is not deemed by academics as a credible source, as it is possible for people to alter information on there. Wikipedia themselves acknowledge this, and would like more academics to be involved in updating their data. However, it is the biggest encyclopaedia online, and can be used as a launch pad to get the basic understanding of a term. Nevertheless, as I have said, this data then needs to be qualified against more traditional academic/rigorous sources.

Secondary data, on the other hand, is often referred to as 'explicit knowledge' and is something everyone has access to – it is in the public domain. Here you will need to say which secondary data you intend to view, and, if I might suggest, you then refer/signpost your reader to Chapter 2 of your thesis where all this data has been put to good use. For example: '(See Chapter 2, to gain a better understanding of how this secondary data has been used.)'.

Primary data

Do not worry here about repetitiveness too much; this is likely to occur in certain sections of your thesis, especially Chapters 1 and 3. Primary data is the knowledge that you are intending to collect for your study, and may be referred to as 'tacit knowledge', which is information that is not in the public domain per se, but is instead held (in the mind) by those you are targeting as your representative sample. The true meaning of tacit knowledge is that which cannot be codified or written down (Bhardwaj and Monin, 2006; Elton, 2010), but is learnt via observation and experience through trial and error. For the section in the proposal, you will be mainly identifying what primary data is and why you intend to collect it. For the chapter in the thesis, it will identify *what* data you have collected and *how* you have collected it.

Strategies

Having discussed your approach, you will now need to consider which strategy(ies) you might wish to adopt in order to undertake your research. As depicted in the research chain in Figure 5.1 above, it can be seen that there are many strategies that could be employed to collect your primary data. You will need to make it quite clear why you have selected certain strategies and how they *fit* with your research (see Quinlan, 2011: on the concept of 'fit'). This means (and I am sorry for using the dirty four-letter word again) that you will have to *read* around these different strategies, and consider different authors' views, so that when the time comes for you to write up your views, you can compare, contrast, and critique them. Therefore, because you have read around them and because you understand the different philosophies and strategies, you will be more comfortable with applying them to your own work. Any good quality textbook or, indeed, journal article will discuss the different strategies. However, in regard to journal articles, they tend to offer a more contemporary viewpoint, whereas textbooks give a good all-round viewpoint (Aunger, 1995; Cohen et al., 2000; Oppenheim, 2001; Smeyers, 2001; Amaratunga et al., 2002; Robson, 2002; Silverman, 2002; de Vaus, 2003; Ryan and Bernard, 2003; Easterby-Smith et al., 2004; Bordens and Abbott, 2005; Saunders et al., 2007; Bryman, 2008; Creswell, 2009; Quinlan, 2011). These different sources do not even scratch the surface of what is out there, or what may be available in your individual institution's libraries, so get onto your library catalogue and look up books and journals connected with research design. You may also wish to visit http://onlineqda.hud.ac.uk/, which will also give you more information on the different philosophies and research methods you can employ in your research design. Remember, you will need to discuss both the advantages and the disadvantages of the strategies/tactics you intend to employ in your research.

Method adoption

As discussed within the philosophies section, you can have a mono or mixed-method approach to your method adoption. In other words, whether you will be adopting a qualitative or quantitative approach to your research, or both – see Teddlie and Tashakkori (2009). Here you will need to think carefully about what it is you are intending to research. For example, if you are fact-finding or simply undertaking observations of what people do, and counting how many times they are doing it, this would be a quantitative approach, fitting with the positivist school of thought. However, if you are seeking peoples' opinions by using interviews and open-ended questions, via face-to-face interviews or a semi- or unstructured questionnaire, or whatever strategy you employ, this will be a qualitative approach. There is nothing wrong in adopting a singular approach, and indeed, might fit better with what it is you are trying to understand.

From the above, you can see that there are two schools of thought – those from a positivistic or quantitative view, and those from an interpretivist/phenomenological or qualitative view. Some researchers within these various schools cannot agree that the other has something to offer; there is a huge amount of material on this particular debate, and it would be easy for you to suffer from writer's drift if you were to try and cover it all. Keep yourself focused, and merely outline to your reader that these two schools of thought exist and that they cannot agree. See the extensive reference list I have provided in the previous section; in particular look at Aunger (1995), Robson (2002) and Amaratunga et al. (2002). Nevertheless, you will need to evidence in your writing that you have a good grasp of the differences between these two approaches/schools, and again evidence the advantages and disadvantages of using each approach.

Some authors (Cohen et al., 2000; Robson, 2002; Saunders et al., 2007) would argue that it is better to adopt a triangulated approach (Teddlie and Tashakkori, 2009) (also referred to as a mixed-method approach) to your research methods; for example, maybe using semi-structured interviews and structured questionnaires and/or focus groups. Having said this, triangulation does suggest a three-way method, as 'tri' means three. Again, you will need to decide which you are going to use and why, and discuss how they *fit* with your research (Quinlan, 2011). As discussed in the philosophies section, this may offer academic rigour, validity, and reliability to your research (Robson, 2002). Whatever you elect to employ for your research, you will need to make it quite clear to the reader why you have chosen this approach and why you have not selected other approaches. Furthermore, do not forget that you will need to discuss the advantages and disadvantages of the approach(es) you finally decided upon.

Sampling

This is one of the key sections in the methodology that you will need to pay particular attention to as you will need to make it explicitly clear how you selected your sample population. If you were to sample the whole population, that would be called a 'census' (Saunders et al., 2007). However, it is highly unlikely that you are going to do this, as it would probably be logistically impossible in the timeframe you have for your study at undergraduate level. It could also be largely dependent on what your sample size consists of. For example, if you are researching views from the top six people in your chosen area, and these are the only people in this field of expertise, this would comprise of a census of the leading minds in that area.

Saunders et al. (2007: p.204) writes:

> *Sampling* [emphasis in original] techniques provide a range of
> methods that enable you to reduce the amount of data you need
> to collect by considering only data from a subgroup rather than
> all possible cases or *elements* [emphasis in original]...[A] full set
> of cases from which a sample is taken is called the **population**
> [emphasis in original].

Therefore, your sample will need to be what is correctly termed a
'representative sample' of your target population; this is a phrase
you should use in your writing as both your first marker and
second marker may be looking for the correct use of research
terminology. As depicted in Figure 5.2, there are various ways of
selecting your sample from the total population. For example,
you could use probability sampling, simple random, stratified
random, non-probability sampling, purposive sampling, and
snowball sampling (Saunders et al., 2007).

What needs to be remembered here is that to use probability
sampling you will need to have access to a full list of the target
population, as the methods under this heading use such
techniques as a lottery – think of the National Lottery – and this
is what they (the authors) are referring to. What this means is
that every person has an equal chance of being drawn from the
population.

Another probability sampling technique is to use a percentage
margin-of-error approach; in other words, 'The margin of error
you can tolerate – that is, the accuracy you require for any
estimates made from your sample' (Saunders et al. 2007, p.210).
The conclusions you draw from this sample of the population
they represent is referred to as 'statistical inference' (Saunders
et al. 2007). Statisticians normally work to a 95% level of
certainty; as such, ' ...this means that if your sample was
selected 100 times, at least 95 of these samples would be certain
to represent the characteristics of the population' (Saunders et
al. 2007, p.211). Many quantitative or statistic books provide you
with lists that give you a rough guide on the percentage margin
of error. Non-probability sampling is used when you do not have
lists, so you have to make a judgment about the sample you are

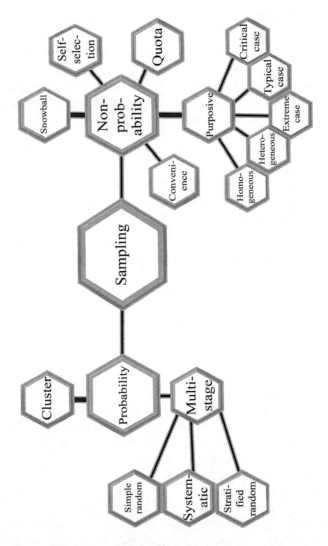

Figure 5.2 Sampling techniques, adapted from Saunders et al. (2007: p.207).

going to collect. This can be done by looking at certain characteristics, such as age, gender, ethnicity, and other elements, but you will need to ensure that you capture people in each element and that each category you are sampling is represented.

Having decided on how you are going to select your sample, you will then need to consider the size of your sample. An accepted norm is for students to try to collect 100 completed questionnaires, and undertake between eight and ten interviews. However, these are only guidelines and as such may change, especially concerning the philosophy and method employed in the research. For example, if the research were purely based on questionnaire collection, we would expect more completed questionnaires. If solely undertaking interviews, we might expect to see a focus group undertaken in addition to the eight to ten interviews. However, in some institutions the tendency might be to encourage a triangulated/mixed-method approach, as this will give students a better 'rounded' experience of undertaking research, and ground them in the skills they might need to employ later in life.

Once more, you will need to explain why you have chosen a particular sampling strategy, and the advantages and disadvantages of using the strategy(ies) adopted. Read various authors' works on this: Cohen et al., 2000; Robson, 2002; de Vaus, 2003; Easterby-Smith et al., 2004; Bordens and Abbott, 2005; Saunders et al., 2007; Creswell, 2009, Teddlie and Tashakkori (2009); Clough and Nutbrown (2012) to name but a few.

Timescale

This falls into two realms: longitudinal and cross-sectional. Longitudinal studies can take the whole lifetime of a researcher; for example, Husserl and Heidegger when studying phenomenology, or a more up-to-date name you may recognise, that of Professor Stephen Hawking.

Cross-sectional research is about the researcher taking a 'snapshot' in time. Many undergraduate studies may fall into this approach. This is mainly because you will have less than one full academic year in which to complete and submit your dissertation. As such, the norm appears to be that most students tend to commence their primary data collection in the last few weeks of term (or semester) one or the beginning of semester two (immediately after the Christmas break). Some students start later, but they should be aware that if they do this, they do not leave themselves much time for analysis and writing up the findings (Chapter 4) and discussion (Chapter 5), and ultimately the conclusions and recommendations chapter (Chapter 6).

In addition to the above, a Gantt chart outlines the time where one activity starts and another finishes (see Figure 5.3).

When looking at my Gantt chart, and in particular the literature review section, you can see that it continues right up until two months before I envisioned handing in my thesis. This should be used as a rough guide and Blu-tacked™ to your wall, close to your computer, to remind you at what stage you are at presently, or what you should be undertaking at what time. The chart you will produce may be more descriptive, offering greater detail. Also, you do not need to set the time as months; you could set it as weeks to make your Gantt chart more focused. The layout of the chart is entirely personal: it is there to guide you, and offer your supervisor an idea of what you should be working on and when. As such, you can use colours or pictures in the cells to help you remember. Some students just produce a table, but I have found that representing this pictorially aids the memory better, and is much easier on the eye. In addition to the above, you need to be realistic in your assessment of the time it will take you, building in some slack period in case you become ill, or if you need to step away from it for a day or two, just to collect your thoughts, and come back to your research with fresh eyes.

Appendix A

A Gantt chart showing the start and end of the different stages in the research

	Sept 2003	Oct 2003	Nov 2003	Dec 2003	Jan 2004	Feb 2004	Mar 2004	April 2004	May 2004	Jun 2004	Jul 2004	Aug 2004	Sept 2004	Oct 2004	Nov 2004	Dec 2004
Literature review	■															■
Questionnaire design						■	■									
Interview schedule design							■									
Pilot of questionnaire								■								
Pilot of interview schedule									■							
Send out questionnaire										■						
Amend interview schedule if necessary											■					
Conduct interviews															■	

	Jan 2005	Feb 2005	Mar 2005	April 2005	May 2005	Jun 2005	Jul 2005	Aug 2005	Sept 2005	Oct 2005	Nov 2005	Dec 2005	Jan 2006	Feb 2006	Mar 2006	Apr 2006
Literature review	■	■	■	■	■	■	■	■				■	■			
Visit interviewees to validate written transcripts								■								
Data analysis									■	■	■	■	■	■		
Write up findings														■	■	■

Figure 5.3 Example of Gantt chart, taken from Feather (2004: p.12).

Data collecting techniques

There are various data collecting techniques that can be employed. The most common one is that of the survey/ questionnaire. What needs to be realised here is that the questionnaire comes in three formats – totally structured, semi-structured, and unstructured – as previously identified, but it is important that you remember these different structures. Why, I hear you saying. Basically, because I have found in my years of supervision across all levels of study – from undergraduate to doctoral – that students write that they are adopting one type of structure for their questionnaire, and then lose focus, producing something that no longer fits with their agenda to meet the study's set objectives.

Totally structured questionnaires are those that have no open-ended questions, and comprise of 'Likert scaling' questions, yes/ no questions, and opinion questions, to name but three.

I often say to my students that a questionnaire cannot be designed in the time it takes to drink a cup of coffee and eat a couple of chocolate digestive biscuits, although they do help sometimes. Much thought and effort needs to go into its design. This research tool has to collect data that will help answer the research objectives you set in your first chapter and repeated at the beginning of the methodology chapter. As such, it needs to be structured in the way it appears so that the questions follow on naturally, the questionnaire is unambiguous to the reader, there are no leading questions, no bias has crept in, it is easy to complete, and it is easy on the eye. I suggest that you use the following book to help you when designing your questionnaire. It is written by Oppenheim (2001) and is entitled: *Questionnaire design, interviewing and attitude measurement.*

Before going live with your questionnaire it is very important to pilot the questionnaire first. You should never, never go and collect primary data without first **piloting** your questionnaire to ascertain if it is working; in other words, that it is collecting the data you need, that it includes everything I have said above, and that it is *coded*.

What do I mean by coded? The questions on the questionnaire need to be either pre-coded or post-coded. Pre-coding is where you can code a question because it is not an open question. For example, it may appear as such:

Q1. Please indicate your gender (Tick one box only):
     Female $\square_1$ Male $\square_2$

Q2. At your last birthday, in which bracket would your age fall? (Tick one box only):
     18-24 $\square_1$ 25-31$\square_2$ 32-38$\square_3$ and so on

Figure 5.4 Example of pre-coding.

Notice in Figure 5.4 that there is a small subscript number to the right of the tick box. This number, the pre-coding, is for your purposes when you are setting up PASW (the old SPSS). Remember, PASW works on numerical data, and once set up correctly can display that numerical data as the label; for example, it will change the '1' to read as female and '2' as male. In addition, notice the layout and how it may be a little easier on the eye, by breaking the text up a little and by using a different colour for the instructions. I acknowledge that the book is printed in black and white, but if you look at Q1 in Figure 5.4 you can discern that the wording in the brackets is slightly greyer; this is because on the original it was in blue. In fact, all the instructions on the questionnaire were written in blue to break up the large chunks of black text. Additionally, the squares for the respondents to tick the answer appropriate to themselves were in a lighter blue than the instructions, thus offering some variation, and therefore easier on the eye. This darker blue colour used throughout the questionnaire will condition your responder that it is for the instructions, and black is for the questions.

The above is fine for a paper-based questionnaire, but today we tend to use online programs such as SurveyMonkey™, Quick Survey™, KwikSurvey™, Google Docs™, and Survey Builder™. However, be careful with some software programs or providers as they tend to have limitations. For example, Survey Monkey will only allow you to receive a set number of responses before you have to start paying for them. Google Docs is free (at the time of writing) and they provide you with a link once your questionnaire is completed. You can then e-mail this link out to people for them to complete your questionnaire. Additionally, you can post the link on such sites as Facebook™ or Twitter™. Some people join a specialist group on LinkedIn™ and place an electronic version of their questionnaire there for completion. Having said this, the electronic questionnaire will not be pre-coded or post-coded; you may have to do this when you enter the data into PASW (SPSS). However, as the data is on a spreadsheet, this should not be a difficult task to undertake. Nevertheless, pre-coding and post-coding are important and you will need to discuss these in your methodology, when discussing questionnaire design.

With post-coding, you have to wait for the questionnaires to come back before you can start analysing the data you have received for any open-ended questions you may have had. You will need to see what answers have been provided and then categorise them under one heading. You will also need to make clear in your findings chapter how you did this and why you chose the 'heading' to represent that or any other category. For example, on your questionnaire, you might ask a question along the lines of 'How does the wearing of perfume make you feel? (Please write your answer in the box provided.)' You might get responses like: fresh; sexy; alluring; clean; attractive to the opposite sex; appealing, etc. From this you might decide on

'Clean' and 'Attractive' as categories for post-coding. These could then break down as follows:

Clean – which includes fresh, will be one category and coded appropriately;

Attractive – this would include attractive to the opposite sex, sexy, appealing.

The codes you would give these variables would follow on from any pre-coded ones you had for the question. If you had no pre-coded answers, then you would start from '1' as with the pre-coding of each question. You may find that you might have to re-code when all the questionnaires have come in, as a new title or term may arise, which means you will need to start again because it does not fit into any of the existing categories you have developed.

Finally, you will need to ensure that your questionnaire carries an ethical statement that indicates who you are, why you are doing the research, what you will get out of it, and how you are going to protect the respondents' rights, including anonymity. In research, we refer to this as 'informed consent'.

If you are undertaking a paper-based questionnaire, the same process is undertaken, but a letter asking for informed consent usually accompanies the questionnaire. Examples of informed consent letters/forms can be found in Robson's (2002) book entitled: *Real World Research*.

Interview schedules

An approach similar to the one you adopted for your questionnaire needs to be employed here. However, you will not pre-code any questions, although, with a semi-structured interview, there may be opportunities for you to do this. Nevertheless, the purpose of an interview is to gain a deeper understanding around some of the topics on your questionnaire, thus allowing you to compare and contrast the findings from the qualitative data with the quantitative data. This in turn may offer more reliability, validity and rigour to your research. As such, interviews tend to be designed to be more flexible, so that the researcher has the freedom to explore any interesting topic/subject that the interviewee may raise whilst being interviewed. See Figure 5.5 below for an example.

Outline of an interview schedule

Read before tape-recording:

Introduction:

The questions below constitute a provisional framework, and the interview will be semi-structured in nature. As such I expect to pursue any unanticipated issues that arise during the process.

The purpose of this study is to look at the perceptions of lecturers delivering HE programmes in Further Education Institutions as to whether or not they perceive themselves to be academics.

Permission has been given by the Principal of the College to approach lecturers to gain their insights and opinions on this subject matter, and I must stress that both you and the college will remain totally anonymous in any written reports growing out of the study, and your responses will be treated in the strictest confidence.

Having said all this, may I have your permission to tape-record the interview, as it will aid in terms of speed, efficiency, and ensuring your responses are accurately recorded and transcribed? I will hand the tape-recorder to you, and if at any time you feel uncomfortable with the interview, please feel free to switch the recorder off. Also, please feel free at any time to interrupt the interview, and ask for clarification of a question or to criticise a line of questioning. Do you understand the ethics of this research?

Main questions	Notes and follow-up questions
Q1. Thank you for agreeing to meet me and to be interviewed. To get the interview started, can you please tell me how many years teaching at FE level you have?	If less than one year, what was their occupation before teaching in FE? Ask to elaborate
Q2. How many years teaching experience do you have at HE level?	
Q3. Do you have any management responsibility?	If yes, what is your level, e.g. pathway leader, course director? If no, ask the respondent to explain their role in HE.
Q4. What are the subject areas you are teaching in?	If they give just one area, ascertain if they are allowed to specialise.
Q5. From the following list, please rank in order what you see as your main role: • Teaching • Researching • Managing • Administration • Writing for publications • Networking	Read through list first, then read again so that respondent can rank them as they are being read.

Figure 5.5 Example of statement for informed consent and an interview schedule (Feather 2009: p.262).

You can also use this schedule to write any additional information or notes on, as the interviewee never sees this piece of paper; it is your aide-mémoire for when it comes to transcribing the recorded interview. This means you can write observations down, such as when they laugh, how long a pause they take before answering, any movement they may make with their arms or hands, and so on. For example, when I asked one of my interviewees to define professionalism, he raised both his arms into the air, looked to the ceiling and almost shouted the words, "Oh my God...No!" (Feather, 2009: p.194).

As with the questionnaire, the interviewee schedule needs piloting, but this may largely be governed by how many people you intend to interview and the size of your sample. This is where your supervisor can be invaluable, as they will have undertaken interviews for their own research and should therefore be able to offer you a real insight into the practicalities. For example, how they structured their schedule and whether the questions gathered relevant and necessary information for them to answer their set research objectives. From this, they will be able to apply this knowledge to your interview schedule and determine whether your questions are leading, ambiguous, worded appropriately, and comply with ethical guidelines.

When you undertake interviews, it is highly recommended that you use a good quality digital recorder to capture the interview. This then will free you up to focus on the questions, write down any interesting points the interviewee makes, so you can re-visit and explore these further, and make notes on your observations of the environment and the body language of your interviewee. However, there are the ethical issues to consider. First, you must ask permission of the interviewee to record the session; most are not averse to this, but some may be, which will mean that you will have to write their narrative verbatim. If you have shorthand writing skills, these will be invaluable for instances such as this. However, if you do not, no worries; you simply will have to do your best to capture as much information as you can. Then, after the interview is concluded and as soon as practicable, when you have found somewhere where you can sit and think, write down the observations that you can remember in your research journal, cross-referencing these observations to the interview, time, and date.

The second ethical issue is that if the interviewee agrees to be recorded, pass the recorder to them to control. This should make them feel more comfortable as they will be in control of the recording, and as such, can stop it if they wish to. This is within their rights as laid down by numerous research ethical bodies and, indeed, may be the same with your own institution.

Focus groups

As with interviews, the same format and procedures are followed in terms of developing the schedule for focus groups. However, focus groups can be extremely difficult to control and as such require much skill on the part of the interviewer (Cohen et al., 2000; Robson, 2002; Saunders et al., 2007). The ideal size of a focus group is between six and ten people (Saunders et al., 2007), but I would recommend taking someone with you to sit outside the circle of the group to take notes on the group's body language, the setting, and any interesting points the group may raise. Obviously, you will need to brief your observer(s) as to what it is you are looking for and on what to pay special attention to when taking notes. This will then free you up to listen intently to what is being said and to notice any signals the group may be giving off. One important aspect is that you will need to ensure that you and your helper are discussing the same person when comparing notes. Draw a seating plan and agree on a numbering system that you can refer to quickly. For example, you might use a system similar to my own, where the seating plan is drawn by both you and your helper, and you agree who is 'focus group member 1' (FGM 1), FGM 2, and so on. That way you will not fall into the trap where you start at one end listing that person as FGM 1, whereas you research assistant might start at the other end referring to the same person as FGM 6. The agreed starting point is usually the first person to the immediate left of the researcher (see Figure 5.6).

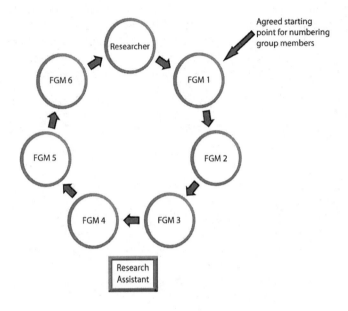

Figure 5.6 Agreed numbering of focus group members.

Observations

This is a very useful and under-used technique employed by many students. Observations fall into two camps: participatory and non-participatory. Taking non-participatory observation first, this is where you do not tell the people you are going to observe them. This can be termed covert observation; for example, you may sit yourself in the library or canteen, and start writing. After a few minutes, the people around you will forget you are there, or may just regard you as another student writing up some notes, when in fact you are taking notes on their body language, behaviour towards one another and other people. In addition, you will be noting their gestures, and any social norms and values that may become apparent – perhaps even what they are saying, but only if it is relevant to your study. You may even make sketches of the environment, or make notes of the lighting, weather, and so on. This is known as offering a 'thick description' of what is occurring (Glaser and Strauss, 1999).

At the other end of the spectrum is participatory observation. Here the person could immerse himself or herself into the culture to gain an understanding of that culture's social norms and values, which could take many years (Spradley, 1979). However, as undergraduate students, or indeed master's students, it is unlikely that this would be an option for you. Therefore, you are more likely to employ 'moderate participation' where you let them know that you are going to be observing them, and get involved to some degree in what is going on. The problem here is that people may alter their behaviour because they know they are being observed.

Observation is also an ethical dilemma, because if you do not tell the individual(s) that they are being observed, this could be deemed unethical; whereas the moderate participative style is seen to be more ethical, as you will have informed the people about to be observed what it is you are doing.

In addition to the above, you may have learned about the Hawthorne Experiment. To cut a long story short, a consultant went into a room where a number of people were working, and no matter what variable was changed, for example, the lighting, the heating, or whatever, production went up. It was concluded that the reason for this was that some people thought the consultant was looking at reducing staffing levels and thus worked harder so as not to lose their job. Others perceived the consultant was looking to earmark who was eligible for promotion and so worked harder (Rollinson, 2005; Mullins, 2006). The conclusion that was reached was that the environment changed because the consultant entered into it. The same applies when you enter into the environment where you are going to undertake your interview; more so if it is at the interviewee's place of work as you, too, will need to consider this factor. Therefore, you may (via your own actions) create some false readings. You should make this transparent when you are writing up your methodology chapter.

There are other data-gathering techniques and you should make yourself fully conversant with what is available; you will also need to ensure that you discuss why you are choosing one method over another. Furthermore, you will need to identify the advantages and disadvantages of using the method you have selected.

You may have noticed I keep writing this, and it is because your supervisor, second marker, and the external examiner will be looking to ascertain if you have grasped the finer nuances of the methods you are adopting, and why.

Rigour

This is an important factor in any research, and you will need to evidence that you have incorporated this into your own research. It refers to the quality of logic you have incorporated into your research design from which you can confidently draw reliable conclusions. Rolfe (2006: p.305) writes, 'Together...verification strategies incrementally and inter-actively contribute to and build reliability and validity, thus ensuring rigor...Rigor is clearly the key to success.' However, what must be remembered is that most of the writing on this refers to the scientific approach, which normally falls under the remit of positivism and the quantitative approaches. When using the qualitative approach, the logical scientific approach should still be considered, but as Rolfe (2006) argues, it is not only down to the researcher to ensure methodological rigour, but also that the reader should be allowed to judge the trustworthiness of the research when examining the dissertation, article, or report.

Ethics

This is a very important part of your methodology because it is here that you will identify your ethical stance in your research; not only the preservation of both the participants' rights but also those of the researcher. The British Education Research Association (BERA, 2004) writes that:

> The Association considers that educational researchers should operate within an ethic of respect for any persons involved directly or indirectly in the research they are undertaking, regardless of age, sex, race, religion, political beliefs and lifestyle or any other significant difference between such persons and the researchers themselves or other participants in the research. (BERA, 2004: p.6)

BERA (2004) further identifies that the intended participants must be fully aware as to why they have been asked to take part in the research, what the research is about, and to whom it is to be reported. You must therefore gain informed consent, and this must be gained before you begin the research with the intended participants. Your own institution where you are studying will have its own research ethics committee and an ethical code of research practices. You will be expected to abide and comply with these codes, as your thesis will belong to the university issuing your degree. Yes, you retain your intellectual property over the thesis, but the institution will hold the copyright.

At my institution, the Research Ethics Committee stipulates that:

> At the heart of all research, regardless of discipline, is the need for researchers to be honest in respect of their own actions in research and in their responses to the actions of others. This applies to the whole range of work, including experimental design, generating and analysing data, publishing results and acknowledging the direct and indirect contributions of colleagues, collaborators and others. All researchers must refrain from plagiarism, piracy or the fabrication of results. In the case of employees, committing any of these actions is

> regarded as a serious disciplinary offence. (Huddersfield University Ethics Committee, 2005: p.2)

Therefore, researchers (students and staff) are expected to observe the standards of good practice set out in your institution's ethical guidelines. You need to ensure that you are fully conversant with these and other professional guidelines on research ethics. It is your responsibility to ensure that you are complying with these guidelines so as not to infringe upon any human rights; for example, that your research will not cause any physiological or psychological harm to the participants.

Limitations

These are factors that you perceive may affect your research and thus limit your ability to conduct research thoroughly; for example, time, access to various people, self-funding, illness, and any other factor that you perceive could stop you conducting your research or interfere with your collection of data for your research. Usually these limitations are those that appeared in your research proposal and are re-stated here. In the analysis chapter of your dissertation, you need a final section entitled 'limitations', where you would list all those factors that have *actually* affected you whilst undertaking your research.

Your 30-second recap

I've taken you through what I deem to be one of the major weak links in the research methodology.

This is the chapter where many students fall down, primarily because they come across words they may not have heard of before.

I've identified that you need a basic understanding of the research philosophies employed.

You must understand the different research techniques that can be employed. More importantly, you need to show how they fit with your individual piece of research.

It's imperative that you apply the same attention to detail in this chapter and others as you do in your literature review.

I've provided models and examples to help you formulate your ideas, and how to put together a Gantt chart and interview schedule.

Re-read this chapter; it's important that you get this right.

Chapter 6: Presenting the results of your labours

Introduction

Now is not the time to panic; you are nearly there. Whilst you have been working on your other chapters, your questionnaires have been working silently in the background bringing in the valuable data that will enable you to draw conclusions and infer what may be occurring in the subject you have decided to study. Your interviews and focus group data is transcribed, and waiting for your careful analysis and interpretation, fair itching to offer up its pearls of wisdom to you to enable you to achieve that all-important grade. So now is the time to reap the rewards of what you have sown.

I will start with the quantitative data first, and then move on to discuss the qualitative data.

Quantitative analysis

I do not intend to produce a chapter on how to calculate statistics, or indeed use statistical software as this is done far better by such authors as Andy Field (2009) in his book *Discovering Statistics using SPSS*. There is also a whole plethora of free tutorials on using SPSS on the Internet; go to Google and type 'Free SPSS (now known as PASW) tutorials' and you will find guides and videos from various credible sources; for example, from some universities in the United States of America and private providers on YouTube. However, be cautious, as some expect you to sign up to their website, so be careful with your selection.

The battle cry of many statisticians is 'show me the data' (Check and Schutt, 2012). However, managers in the commercial sector also need this evidence, so being able to analyse what you have gathered is a good skill to learn, possibly even to master.

Whether in academia or the commercial sector, there will come a time when '...you will need to figure out what the piles of data you have gathered all mean – what story do they tell?' (Check and Schutt, 2012: p.275). Do not get confused with the 'story' aspect of the quote, as this is usually a phrase used in qualitative data. Nevertheless, like all data, statistics, as factual as they may be, are only factual up until the point they are interpreted by the individual. At this point, values, beliefs, stereotyping, and many other issues may influence the researcher interpreting the data. However, that is another story.

When you are undertaking quantitative data analysis, you will need to make it very clear to the reader exactly what it is you are analysing and why (Robson, 2002). You need to walk your reader through the data you are offering up as evidence, and inform them exactly what that evidence is showing. You will also need to be as objective as you can, putting your own personality and beliefs to one side when you analyse the data. I know what your next question is: 'How can I leave my individuality to one side?' The answer is simple: you cannot. However, by en-deavouring to be objective, you are evidencing that you are trying to offer academic rigour to your research and its findings. As Roberts (2010: p.158) identifies, you will need to '...report the descriptive or inferential statistical tests and procedures you used, how they were treated, and the level of statistical significance that guided your analysis'. Buckingham and Saunders (2004: p.13) further identify that when undertaking quantitative research you need to consider the '3 A's', that is, people's Attributes, Attitudes, and Actions. Attributes are to do more with demographics, their gender, age, and occupation, whereas attitudes are to do with their values and beliefs, for example, how they feel about something – perhaps drinking. Actions are whether they are involved in the activity, that is, do they drink themselves (Buckingham and Saunders, 2004).

To this end, you need to be quite clear about how you are going to address each question, and the tests you intend to use (Roberts, 2010; Check and Schutt, 2012). See the works of Field (2009), Saunders et al. (2009), and Thomas et al., (2011), who give some very good worked examples and exercises using different statistical calculations for you to follow and work through.

Structure

This part is important. You need to sit down and give some thought as to how you intend to present your findings to your reader; that is, what order the tables and graphs are going to appear in. Most students tend to produce the tables and graphs in line with how the questions appear on the questionnaire. However, you need to think about what data you need to present first, not how it appears on your questionnaire (Roberts, 2010). It may be that you first present all the data that answers your first research objective, then the second objective, and so on. Whichever way you decide, it will need to be presented in a structured and logical format and in the correct tone for the intended reader.

Most students tend to make a common mistake when presenting tables and graphs: they forget to number them and provide a title. For example, let us say you are now ready to present your first table in Chapter 4, and you are evidencing the gender ratio of your sample; the number and title would appear thus: 'Table 4.1 Gender'. The '4' represents the chapter, the '1' denotes that it is the first table in that chapter; the title is self-explanatory. Each table thereafter will run consecutively.

The same procedure is used for graphs (which are usually labelled as Figures or Fig.). We term graphs as figures as they usually denote a pictorial image of what is appearing in the table. Again, the figures would run consecutively. Using our gender example again, it would appear in the chapter as 'Fig. 4.1 Gender'. Yes, you have guessed it: the '4' denotes the chapter and the '1' represents, in this case, that it is the first graph used in that chapter.

From the above, it may be useful to produce all your tables (tables are still labelled 'Table', for example, 'Table 3.1') and graphs first before you commence your analysis and summary of each table and graph (Roberts, 2010). You can then decide more easily which order you wish your tables and graphs to appear in, and move them around and renumber them until you have the structure you are looking for. This will also allow you to decide which tables and graphs you wish to present in the chapter, and which may be better presented in the appendices. All that is left to do then is to analyse the content of the table and/or graph you include in the body of the thesis. Roberts (2010) suggests that you can further structure your tables and graphs chronologically by variables: by themes, by hypotheses, by patterns, and by research questions. The latter is not the questions that appear on the questionnaire, but the research questions for which you are trying to provide answers.

Readers

Another aspect of your chapter, and indeed for the whole dissertation, is the tone you write in. This means you will have to write for your audience, very much as I am writing for you now. It is a hard balance to make. The reason being is that you know that your supervisor, the internal moderator, and the external examiner may know the subject area on which you are researching and writing your thesis. However, you also need to evidence your knowledge to these same people, so how do you do that? I am afraid there is no real easy answer to this. I always tell my students to explain everything, and write as if the person does not know the subject. Remember what I have said in previous chapters: your supervisor is there to guide you through the process, but they may have only a working knowledge of the area that you are studying. Moreover, because you are focusing in on the subject, you may become more knowledgeable than your supervisor, internal examiner, and indeed the external examiner are.

Having discussed the above, what you need to remember here is that you are merely stating the facts that appear in the tables and graphs: nothing more, nothing less. On this, Roberts (2010: p.171) reminds us that '...the findings from your study should be presented objectively and without editorializing or speculating – free from author bias'.

Quality of analysis

I cannot stress enough the care that you must take when analysing and reporting your data. You will need to ensure that you have interpreted the data correctly; as such, you will need to double-check your results and then, for good measure, check them again. Another option would be to ask your supervisor if she or he would be willing to check them over for you. However, I draw your attention to the fact that they may not have the time. Remember, they have other commitments and other students to look after so do not be disappointed if they say no. This is not them being awkward or unhelpful; it is purely that they have to manage their time and may have heavy teaching loads and/or administration duties to perform. You should make full use of the academic skills tutors or learning development group resources, as these people are given time to help you with a whole plethora of skills, including statistical analysis and the use of PASW (formerly SPSS). Over the years I have learnt, especially with some international students, that students believe they will 'lose face' if they approach these people for help. This is not the case; there is no shame in asking for guidance. As a manager, you would not think twice about using such a valuable resource, so use it.

At the end of the day, what is crucial here is that the analysis of your data is correct and that you have double-checked your results. These results must be accurately reported and free from bias or erroneous interpretation; otherwise you may jeopardise all the hard work you have undertaken in collecting the data, and as such, the reliability and validity of your research.

Qualitative analysis

Like the quantitative analysis section above, I do not intend to give a blow-by-blow account on how to analyse qualitative data using the various software programs out there, such as 'NU:DIST' or 'NVivo'. There are various training guides offered on Google; just type in 'How to use NVivo' and you will see a number of guides and tutorials from around the world that will become available to you, some of which are visual representations on YouTube from QSR, the developers of NVivo.

This qualitative software program allows you to code and tease out similarities in the transcriptions from your recorded interviews. You identify the similarities and then assign them a code – see Charmaz (2014) on how to code qualitative data; alternatively Silverman (2002) offers different approaches to undertaking this task. However, I have to say that, in my opinion, NVivo is not an easy program to master in the time you have available to complete your undergraduate thesis. As such, I recommend that you keep it simple and stick to content analysis and the teasing out of themes (Dawson, 2009), using quotes from your respondents to support your argument (Hennink et al., 2011), and to compare and contrast with your quantitative research (if you are using a mixed-method or triangulated approach). LeCompte (2000) suggests breaking your analysis up, somewhat akin to a jigsaw puzzle where you separate out the different pieces (edge pieces, sky, and so on). You can then start constructing your 'jigsaw puzzle' in a clear methodical way.

Qualitative observations

The above does not mean that you cannot produce tables and graphs from qualitative research; you can. For example, you could produce a graph that shows the number of times a certain word or phrase was used. You could then compare this to other variables, such as the gender of your interviewees, their age, their experience, or any other demographic or geographic variable relevant to your research. I would suggest that you put a copy of your transcriptions in your appendices and highlight to the reader how these themes, phrases, or words were categorised and identified. Earlier, I discussed other ob-servations that you should record; this will provide your reader with a picture of the situation in which the interview took place. Why should you do this? Well, it is simple: the reader was not there, so by painting them a picture (using words) they can contextualise how the interviewees' comments fit together – the jigsaw analogy again fits here. That is, you are assembling the pieces, and then developing the picture by placing each piece in its respective place.

When analysing qualitative data, it is not as easy as it first may seem. As Teddlie and Tashakkori (2009: p.250) observe, *'Qualitative data analysis* [emphasis in original] is the analysis of various forms of narrative data, including data stored in audio, [DVD], and other formats.' Qualitative data is normally viewed as being grounded in the inductive domain (Teddlie and Tashakkori, 2009), or as Denzin and Lincoln (2003: p.5) argue:

...qualitative research involves an interpretive, naturalistic approach to the world. This means that qualitative researchers

> study things in their natural settings, attempt to make sense of, [sic] or to interpret, phenomena in terms of the meanings people bring to them.

This means that they will let the theory come from the findings and observations or, as we have discussed above, adopt an inductive approach. Denzin and Lincoln (2003) go on to argue that:

> ...qualitative researchers deploy a wide range of interconnected interpretive practices, hoping always to get a better understanding of the subject matter at hand. It is understood, however, that each practice makes the world visible in a different way. Hence, there is frequently a commitment to using more than one interpretive practice in any study. (Denzin and Lincoln, 2003: p.5)

Having discussed the above, like quantitative data, qualitative data also needs to be presented and written in a structured way that is logical, well argued, and coherent, and uses a methodical approach – like the analogy of the jigsaw puzzle by LeCompte (2000) mentioned earlier.

Making an argument

Students often ask me what this phrase means exactly. Hennink et al. (2011: p.277) explain this quite well when writing that, 'An argument is the construction of a perspective, a line of reasoning or the development of an exploration, which is based on analysis of your data.' All writing conveys an argument in one way or another, through either discussion or analysis, or both. There are different types of argument that you can employ in your work: for example, developmental, mechanical, comparative, and causal (Hennink et al., 2011).

Developmental is self-explanatory: it is where you will explain how the processes develop. One example of this could be your literature review, where you explain how concepts and theories may have developed over time. Another example is the processes you have used to analyse your data in your findings chapter, and the different variables you may have compared and why.

A mechanical argument is an attempt to explain how things work. An example of this could be your research methodology, explaining how the processes and methods you intend to adopt work with your proposed research. Again, here, it would be explaining how the different statistical tests work, and describing the formulae you have used to analyse the data. The same applies with the qualitative data if you are using NVivo or content analysis: what type of coding did you use; was it numbers or narrative?

Comparative arguments are the comparing and contrasting of different core themes in order to develop an argument. Again, this could be undertaken in your literature review, but it is most likely that you will apply these core themes to your overall discussion in Chapter 6 when addressing your research question(s) and objectives. Nevertheless, here, in this chapter, it would be the comparison of different variables to ascertain if there is a cause and effect, or if there is any significance, even if you are using simple descriptive statistics. With the qualitative data, you can compare different narratives to ascertain if the respondents are using the same terminology, or whether they use different phrases for the same meaning; for example, some people use 'leader' and 'manager' interchangeably, even though they are quite different. I will discuss the example of customer relationship marketing (CRM) later in this chapter.

Unlike quantitative data, qualitative data can and does produce vast quantities of rich data, which needs to be gone through, line by line, and sentence by sentence. This is not to say that quantitative data does not produce vast amounts of data, but, if you have a thousand questionnaires and all the data is entered into the software program you have elected to use, all the data can be reduced down to one number. For example, if you test for a significance between two given variables, the number that the computer will generate will be either greater or lesser than 0.05. It would be difficult to write a chapter on that number alone.

Having said this, with qualitative data you cannot report on everything you produce (Hennink et al., 2011); plus it is very easy to get lost in the reams of paper that will carry all your data if you were to produce everything. To provide you with an example, for my doctorate I conducted 26 individual interviews, each of an hour's duration, and each interview was tape-recorded with the permission of the interviewee. The average time to transcribe an hour-long interview is around ten hours. However, if the individual has a guttural dialect, or is from another country, the time to transcribe can multiply considerably. From these interviews, I produced 26 transcripts, each comprising of 25 or more typed A4 pages of narrative. It is thus imperative that you remain focused at this time and are not disturbed. This is because you will need to tease out the common themes and word usage that your respondents have offered up in their interview with you. From this, you will then be able to weave together a narrative that conveys an overall picture of their lived experiences. One piece of advice I will give you is that you should transcribe your interview data as soon as practicable. The reason being is that if you leave them all until the end (as I did), transcribing them can become a laborious and monotonous process; one which you may find yourself procrastinating over, rather than getting on with it. Believe me when I tell you, that the ironing looked more appealing at times than writing up the transcripts; it is here that you may need to draw deep on those reserves you have, and practise what one of my second-year students once said to me about reading – "You just have to power through it".

A causal argument is based around the idea of cause and effect. It looks at why certain phenomena occur in certain situations and not in others. For example, why do some students who obtained an A* in English at school produce work for university in their first year that shows they are unable to string two sentences together using the correct grammar, or have a poor command of the English language in terms of written communication.

Contrary to quantitative data, qualitative data can provide you with a number of different audiences (Hennink et al., 2011) that you are writing for. To this end, your writing needs to be transparent, and you will need to 'signpost' the reader backwards and forwards to different chapters and sections in your thesis. This will evidence that you are linking vital parts together, and will save you the time and effort of having to write out the same material, thus being in fear of repeating yourself. However, it is accepted that a certain amount of repetition may occur in certain chapters, but not much. As Hennink et al. (2011) highlight, you will need to inform the reader where to go and why they need to go there. This is good practice, not just for this chapter but also for the other chapters in your thesis.

Quoting participants

When you use your participants' narratives as quotes, do not just write what they said word for word. To do this would leave out that all-important element you wish to capture – their personality. Your transcriptions would be devoid of all emotion and identity of the individual you thought necessary to interview to give you the depth of insight you wished to gain and learn about a particular point or points. The unspoken word can be just as important as the spoken word, so reproduce the imagery you observed because your reader was not there. For example, give important information that is necessary to provide the reader with a picture, without giving so much away that you jeopardise your participants' anonymity. To give you a working example, in my research I provided the gender, the number of year's experience they had in their occupation, and any managerial or administrative duties they had.

Further to the above, if a participant pauses for any length of time before answering the question, or whilst answering the question, make a note of how many seconds they paused for, and then write at that point in the narrative how long they paused. For example: 'When asked to define professionalism, Interviewee (Int.) 1 stated "I should know the answer to that, I recently undertook an assignment on it [7 second pause], is it...?"' The pause is just as important as the spoken word, in that, depending on the body language that accompanies the pause, it could be that the interviewee is having to think about it, or worse, does not know the answer and is trying to provide what they perceive as a plausible definition. If you believe this latter point to be the case, draw the reader's attention to it, and leave it up to the reader to decide; remember, at this point you are still being objective. I used to use a full stop to represent each second of pause; however, after further reflection and practice, I now use the above method. The reason for this is that if you have to use an ellipsis (...) in the middle of a quote as well as noting where the interviewee has paused, it can become both confusing and messy.

To provide an example, I have used a quote from my thesis. Here I asked the interviewee what the term 'academic' meant to them; Int. 17 said that the term 'academic' was:

> ...to do with [4-second pause] I suppose it's [6-second pause], I suppose I see the word as [to] do [with], that deep, deeper, more, you know, fundamental learning [6-second pause] as in FE [6-second pause] I always have this feeling we're [5-second pause] [we] have a tendency, because of time, to sort of just skim the surface; we don't go deep enough. (Feather, 2009: p.168)

To kill two birds with one stone, as the saying goes, I have used the same quote below to show how the quote would look using a full stop to represent each second the interviewee paused, and in relation to the following discussion.

Also, include words such as 'erm', or 'err'. Some people may be against this, but I (as a qualitative researcher) would say that it

111

provides a rich picture of the person you are interviewing. For instance, in a paper I wrote, I included such terms and even colourful metaphors that the interviewee had used. The anonymous reviewer argued I made the interviewees 'sound thick'. This is not the case, and I argued this with the journal's editor that what I offered was an unadulterated rich account of what the person said, thus allowing the reader to see that which they could not see: the personality of the person I was interviewing. These people were far from the stereotype the reviewer employed; they were all very intelligent people, and what I depicted was how these lecturers lived and behaved in the environment that they worked in. Here are a couple of examples of quotes from my doctoral thesis that I wrote on academic identities, where Interviewee (Int.) 17 felt the term 'academic' was:

> ...to do with....I suppose it's......I suppose I see the word as [to] do [with], that deep, deeper, more, you know, fundamental learning......as in FE......I always have this feeling we're.....[we] have a tendency, because of time, to sort of just skim the surface of things; we don't go deep enough. (Feather, 2009: p.168)

The first thing you may observe from the above quote is the number of pauses the interviewee makes of varying lengths of between four and six seconds, where each full stop equates to one second in time. Where you see '...' (as at the beginning of the quote above), this is what is called an 'ellipsis', which means that some words have been left out purposefully. However, given what I wrote above about using square brackets and recording the length of pause, if you feel the second example looks better with the full stops to represent the length of pause, then undertake this form of description. Therefore, if the ellipsis is in the middle of the sentence, it means that words not relevant to the discussion have been missed out in order to join two sentences together to make sense. So as to avoid confusion, do not record three-second pauses, because they are not relevant as the time is so short, but past this, the pause starts to get a little long, or what people may call a 'pregnant pause'.

The next thing you will notice is the use of colloquial English: can't, it's and we're. This is part of the individual's personality and should not be corrected (in my opinion), as it offers a rich insight into their (the interviewee's) identity. The words in the square brackets are words I have added to help the reader understand what it is the individual is trying to say, without influencing the richness of the narrative too much.

Another example, from a different interviewee (Int. 8), but this time on a core theme that came out of reading various texts on academic identity within further education (FE) (and from a large majority of those I interviewed) was that of 'Jack of all trades'. On this, Int. 8 stated:

> We are Jack[s] of all trades, definitely, and it's often said if you go into FE you might come in as a specialist...and you might spend ten per cent of your time on your specialism...After about two years [teaching at the college], you'll teach bloody anything (laughs). (Feather, 2010: p.197)

With this example, you can see the differences straightaway from the first example: the sentence is more coherent and the individual obviously has knowledge of the theme being explored. For instance, there are not as many pauses, and the colourful metaphor that the individual uses is clearly part of their personality, as they feel comfortable expressing this in front of a person they have met for the first time. Also, notice how I give the reader an insight to this personality by including in brackets that, during the interview, the individual laughs after they had sworn, which indicates that, although the individual may not like the situation they see themselves in, they make light of it. One could read from this that the individual is maintaining their good spirits and positive view on their working life, despite their specialism possibly being viewed as somewhat diluted. As Hennink et al. (2011: p.229) writes, 'These subtle details may be lost when simply describing the issues without using the participants' words directly.'

A further consideration to bear in mind when writing up your findings is not to use jargon (Strauss, 2003). By using jargon you run the risk of your reader turning against your work because they cannot understand it (Strauss, 2003). Always explain any jargon that you may have to use the first time it is used. For example, I used 'Int.' as a shortened version of 'Interviewee', hence the first time I used it, it appeared as 'Interviewee (Int.)', and thereafter as 'Int.'. Most theories comprise of some jargon; for example, if you used the letters 'CRM' without any explanation, the reader could interpret them as Customer Relationship Marketing, or Customer Retention Management, or Critical Risk Management, or something else entirely. Always, always explain acronyms or shortened words; do not leave your readers in the dark.

Your 30-second recap

I've discussed both quantitative and qualitative analysis, and provided you with some examples from my own thesis.

I've purposefully not lingered on analysing and reporting quantitative data, as there are authors' works out there (examples of which I've provided).

I've focused on reporting qualitative data.

Qualitative data has software that can be used for analysis, but at this point in your studies it's not easy to learn.

Report exactly what your interviewees say to you. To me this is important, as it is to other authors such as Hennink et al. (2011).

Remember that you must report the facts as they appear: nothing less, nothing more. If you don't, this could place your research in jeopardy in terms of its rigour, reliability, and validity.

Be transparent on how you've arrived at your findings and what statistical calculations you've used and why.

Read LeCompte's (2000) article entitled *Analyzing Qualitative Data* (see bibliography for full reference).

Chapter 7: Time to shine

Introduction

It is now time to get to the practical details, the facts, the job at hand, and the telling of the story. Having discussed and worked through everything above, you are now like a well-maintained, thinking and writing machine, and ready to focus on exactly what you wish to tell your reader. This is the all-important chapter the reader has being itching to read; the discussion chapter. Some cannot bear the long wait and jump straight to it; others like to get there in their own time, soaking up what you have written, letting you take them by the hand and guide them through the story. Do not disappoint them now; this is your time to shine.

When it comes to writing this chapter, some students say to me that they do not know where to begin, even with having accomplished everything up to this point. Sound familiar? The simple answer is: at the beginning, of course. When I wrote this last sentence, I envisioned you pulling a face or saying something like "Tell me something I don't know". But if you think about it seriously, I just did tell you something you did not know. The question: where do I begin? The answer: at the beginning! Your response should have been, "What do you mean by the beginning?" The beginning, like all your previous chapters, commences with an introduction. The last time your reader read what you intend to do with your research was in Chapter 1, so now would be a good time to **re-introduce** them to the research question, the aim of the research, and the objectives and/or the hypotheses you intend to measure or test.

Objectives as headings

At undergraduate level, I get my students to use their objectives as headings. By adopting this approach, it will keep you focused on the task. As such, you know that you will have to pull in information from previous chapters to put forward an argument (story) that compares, contrasts, and critiques different views on the subject relating to the objective, what methods you employed to answer this objective, and what the findings showed – how they fit together. Remember the jigsaw analogy? You then have to write how the objective or hypothesis was proved or disproved, and how your data supports this. You will need to make this very clear to your readers.

Use the objective again in the sentence. For example, if the objective was to 'Determine if leadership and management are one and the same', you may commence your concluding sentence as follows (first focusing on the leadership aspect):

'From the above discussion and the evidence provided (see sections 2.5, 2.7, and 2.10; also see tables 4.10, 4.11, and 4.12; also see Fig. 4.10, 4.11, 4.12, 4.13, and 4.14) it has been made explicitly clear that there is a fundamental difference between the two terms and their definitions. For example, in the literature review it was shown that X (citation) identified that leadership comprised of Y. This is supported by the research findings (see Table 4.12 and Fig. 4.14) where 70% of the respondents agreed with this statement. This was further evidenced from the interviews when Int. P stated "…". Furthermore, some ambiguity may arise from different authors using the terms interchangeably when discussing them. This was evident when Z showed that leadership was more in line with management when arguing "…" (see section 2.20 and 2.21). This was in line with 42% of the respondents' beliefs. From this we can see that there is some confusion in the minds of a number of the respondents as some of these elected to answer

Q.12 which provided the 70% result, identified above. This is further evidenced when Int. T stated that "...".'

In addition to the above, you will need to discuss and highlight any contradictions that you may have unearthed. Moreover, how these contradictions may have an effect upon your research. Furthermore, you will need to evidence and highlight any unexpected findings from your research. As Roberts (2010: p. 179) highlights:

> Provide the reader with your analysis of the unusual problems or surprising outcomes. You may choose to include this information in various sections or create a separate section to discuss these findings.

This is good advice, but in my opinion I would include it in the section under the objective you are discussing, where the unusual or surprising finding occurred, therefore keeping the evidence and discussion together. Remember to remain focused on the section you are discussing; do not drift.

For each objective and/or hypothesis, you should apply the above approach. Be clear about what it is you are telling the reader; provide evidence and data from your literature review and primary data findings; be objective in your approach, highlighting any unusual and/or surprising findings for each section.

In each section, you should also identify any new knowledge you have discovered, and how it may influence the way the chosen topic is going in the future. Above all, be transparent; do not hide data because you disagree with it, or because it is out of kilter with what you believe. Be open; present the data with good objective analysis and supporting evidence, and let the reader decide. This is what research is about; it is about presenting an informed argument based on sound ethical findings and good analysis, which includes any anomalies you have unearthed.

The EOI of research

Having provided you with a worked example above for formulating your discussions, it may prove prudent to remember Walcott's (2001) examination, observation, and interview (EOI) concept of qualitative research when writing up. He discusses these from an archival research perspective, but I see no reason why they cannot be applied to any writing up of research.

Examination

Here, as I have shown above, you would produce what it is you have discovered from your examination of literature, based upon the concepts, theories, and subject you have elected to research.

Observations

This relates to the observations you have made in your interviews, or simply by observing people's behaviour in a given situation. As I showed you in the previous chapter, introduce these observations into your narrative again; for example, my respondent who swore and laughed; the body language, the observation of their expressions, or indeed the surroundings they are in at the time. This is where your research journal will be invaluable, if you have been recording your observations throughout your journey. For example, when you have finished your interview, you should immediately record (or as soon as practicable) any observations you make. One of my experiences will suffice nicely here.

I had just concluded an interview with a female participant in a college that was set in beautiful countryside, with well-manicured lawns leading up to what, at first glance, could easily pass as a corporate reception area. The interviewee had come to meet me at the designated time for the appointment, and I was escorted down a long, narrow path to some classrooms where the interview was to be conducted. Entering the classroom was like stepping back in time; it reminded me of my schooldays. There was an old-fashioned revolving rubber blackboard, dusty from the leftover residue of chalk that had been used in lessons past. There were some signs of modernity in the classroom in the form of a whiteboard and an overhead projector. The room smelt musty but welcoming, despite there not being much light, and we sat facing each other across a desk that many a student will have sat at over time. However, before I get too lost in my memories, let us move the story along. It was when I had concluded the interview and was returning to my car that I noticed two men having a heated debate. As I drew near, I could make out the gist of their conversation, and was both amazed and excited to learn that they were discussing a point I had raised in the interview with the woman interviewee in the musty classroom. They lowered their voices as I approached, and I quickly got into my car (in the passenger seat nearest to them), set my papers on top of the dashboard, and started to write up my thoughts in my research journal; or that is how it may have appeared to the men debating. I wound my window down (I know, I am a devil, aren't I), and started to listen (I could hear them quite clearly). It was not long before they had forgotten that I was sitting there; to them, I was merely someone writing down some notes. However, I was actually taking key notes and observations of their discussion. Why did I do this? The answer is two-fold really. First, what they were saying was totally out of kilter with what the woman interviewee had said to me earlier. Second, because I was capturing 'rich data' from people in the sector who had knowledge on the subject, and the information I was collecting was not biased as I had not altered their environment. (I draw your attention here to the Hawthorne Experiment, which I mentioned earlier.) The above data was captured in 2008, and I am only able to share my experiences of the interview, the day, and of what I recorded because I had my research journal to hand to take notes of my observations.

Interviews

The data you capture in your interviews, if you have planned these well and captured the relevant data you need to answer your research objectives, will be invaluable. It should be understood that all the above elements need to be woven together (with your quantitative analysis) to form a clear, coherent record of the events that transpired. The information you have unearthed needs to either support or refute your research question; that is, prove or disprove your hypotheses, and/or provide you with the opportunity to evidence whether your objectives and research question have been answered or not. Unlike quantitative data, interviews allow you to bring your research to life, as I said earlier, by evidencing your observations and the interviewee's personality. As Smith et al. (2009: pp. 108-109) observe:

> You may have captured that process with various devices along the way. However, your reader was not alongside you during that process and therefore you must present your results in a full narrative account, which is comprehensible, systematic, and persuasive to that reader who is coming to your study for the first time...Your analysis of your participants' sense-making is of no value unless your reader can make sense of it too!

Confidence in writing

When it comes to writing up your discussion, you must have confidence in both your ability to write well and in your analytic abilities (Strauss, 2003). As Strauss (2003: p.260) identifies, '...the issue here is not whether the analysis has been adequately and sufficiently done, but confidence that one really knows the answers to those questions'.

Strauss (2003) is not playing down the importance of good analysis, but is emphasising that the student must be confident that when writing up their discussions and subsequent analysis, they have answered the set research question, addressed the research objectives, and has proved or disproved any set hypotheses. For example, a good friend of mine once said (and I have iterated this previously in other chapters) that it is just as important to show that you have tried to disprove a hypothesis, as well as endeavouring to prove it. As Habermass (1987) highlights, when it comes to epistemological knowledge, there are two realms: there is the epistemological knowledge of 'knowing' and 'absolute' epistemological knowledge. That is, we know what we know through research and experimentation now, but we do not know everything, we do not have all the answers: we do not have absolute knowledge. Even when you have concluded your research, you will not know everything there is to know or to learn on the subject; you know what you have unearthed from what you have already read (secondary research), and from your primary research. Nothing more, nothing less. Even the greatest thinkers of our time do not know everything, so take some solace in that. What I am saying here, and what I have said many times before, is just report what you have found from your reading, observations, and primary research.

From what I have written above, you should apply this approach to research question(s), each of your objectives, and each of your hypotheses. This chapter is the chapter that pulls everything together so be thorough: check you have addressed everything you set out to address, get a draft to your supervisor for formative feedback in good time – not at the last minute – and please, please, please, check for errors and typographical mistakes.

Conclusions and recommendations

Now that you have written your discussion chapter, it is now time to write the final chapter (Chapter 6) of your thesis. This is where you will pull out the **key points or findings** you have discovered when conducting, analysing, and discussing your research.

Conclusions

It is very important in this section that you ensure that you are linking the data you have found and discussing how you have addressed the research question. I have given examples earlier in the book where students have lost valuable marks due to their conclusions not relating to the research data they have discussed, or indeed the research topic under investigation. All the way through the writing up of your thesis, you should be constantly checking that you have not entered in to 'writer's drift', and that you have remained focused on what it is you are researching, why you are researching it, and what is the knowledge you are trying to evidence. This is important, as you will be sharing your new found knowledge with the academic community and/or the commercial sector; furthermore, it is a tangible piece of research that you can show any prospective employer to evidence that you have the necessary skills to conceptualise and develop a project through to fruition. As an undergraduate student, you are not expected to find 'new-to-the-world' knowledge, but if you do, great! If you do not, that is no problem either, as your knowledge will add to the pot of existing knowledge, and may open up a new path for further exploration.

When you are concluding, be careful about over-generalisation, more so if your target sample is not a complete representative sample of the population being studied. It may be better to err on the side of caution and make inferences rather than generalisations. By doing this, you are saying that it could be the same elsewhere, but not definitively saying it is. Revisit the section on sampling and read around the subject in more detail to be certain you understand about generalising and inferring.

Again, make it clear how you have addressed the research question, and how your research objectives have been addressed.

Finally, remember that this is the chapter where you will be pulling out the key findings to put forward a discussion based on these key findings. It is where you come off the fence and state clearly what your research has uncovered, and that it has answered the research question from your perspective. Additionally, you may find that you have not fully answered the objectives, and subsequently the research question; to this end, you would then need to put forward recommendations as to what needs to be undertaken to bring this about.

Recommendations

These usually come in the form of six bullet points, identifying what should be undertaken in the future; these you will recognise as you complete your thesis. I have graded some students' work where they have written paragraph upon paragraph of recommendations; sometimes they have written more in this part than they have in their conclusions. Stick to the brief; that is, the guidelines set by your institution. If you are uncertain, check with your supervisor.

Your 30-second recap

I've given you an idea of how your discussion chapter should proceed.

I've told you what you need to show, and why. I've provided you with an example of my observations and a way to express these to the reader (in this case, you).

I've given you a worked example of weaving together an observation into a discussion.

I've also identified to you that you're only human. Don't try to know it all; you won't be able to accomplish this.

Focus on knowing what you've read, what you've observed, and what you've found out from your primary data. This is your knowledge of the here and now. The time is ripe to show this to your readers, whoever they may be.

I've evidenced how there should be no holes in your analysis for people to pick up on; be tight on your analysis, making sure you've covered what it was you set out to do.

Signpost the reader back to other chapters and sections within those chapters as required to aid you in pulling the story together.

There are numerous books and articles on quantitative analysis, and if this is your preference, then you should read the following works: Cochran et al., 1954; Adcock, 1989; Fowler Junior, 1992; Cummings, 1998; Bordens and Abbott, 2005; Field, 2009; Saunders et al., 2009; Teddlie and Tashakkori, 2009; Thomas et al., 2011.

Chapter 8: Craftsmanship – now comes the hard bit

Introduction

The time has come to stop writing and start your quality control checks. Your thesis is before you on the computer screen and you need to commence editing. Here you need to be critical of yourself, looking at your work with a discerning eye.

This aspect of the work is just as important as all the other work you have undertaken to get to this point; do not run out of steam now. If you have not left enough time, then sorry, it may be too late for you to do this; but you should still try, even if it means working up to the last minute before getting it in to be bound. If you have left yourself enough time, use this now to your advantage: polish your thesis to a highly professional piece of work.

Proofreading

Saunders et al. (2009) advises that your friends peer review your work to offer you some critical feedback. However, my internal alarm goes off when I read this. For me, giving your friends a copy of your work to look at is too close to plagiarism. It is too much of a carrot to dangle in front of a friend, especially if they are behind with their dissertation and are working on something similar to you. Therefore, my advice would be not to do this so that you are not placing yourself in a situation where you might be infringing your university's guidelines and policies on what constitutes plagiarism to them. Universities usually have someone who can aid you with your proofreading skills, if you have allowed sufficient time. Additionally, there is an option to pay a professional proofreader to do this, but this may be expensive, and again, they would require a certain amount of 'lead time' to do this. Your supervisor may be able to guide you here. If not, go and see your learning development group or academic skills tutor (whichever your university refers to these lecturers as), as they will definitely be able to advise you.

Word count

If you are over the word count, you will need to go through your thesis sentence by sentence, checking for any material you could get rid of that is not relevant, or seeing if you could write a sentence in another way, using fewer words. For example, if you find you are using a phrase such as 'higher education' on numerous occasions, on the first use of the phrase place '(HE)' in brackets afterwards. Then you can continue with just the initials and you will have reduced two words to one.

Typos, sentence structure, grammar and punctuation

The number of dissertations I mark where I see these errors always amazes me, especially as I drum it into students in the workshops, lectures, and seminars I hold to check for this before they submit me a draft of a chapter. Why am I amazed? Because even though they corrected the draft, the final version (on some occasions) seems to contain the same errors that I suggested they may wish to correct on the first draft. You will lose marks for these types of errors. In addition, the more the lecturer reads and picks up on these errors tends to (in my opinion) put them off reading the rest (although they have to in order to provide you with a grade). Your supervisor will have a large number of dissertations to read which will include those she or he did not supervise. Imagine, if the supervisor has just read the worst dissertation in the lot given to him/her, then they commence reading yours and on the first page there are a number of typos, grammar mistakes, and sentence structure errors. Do you think they are going to be impressed? I doubt it. My pet hate is when students use 'text' language in their writing, for example, 'It might be that u look at...' or '...I 2 like u think that...'. Arghhh! The worst example I have had is 'LOL' at the end of a sentence; this one in particular really grinds my gears. Save this type of writing for your friends on your mobile telephone. Remember, you are supposed to be a student practitioner, so be professional: write to the best of your abilities to the academic standard required.

Editing

Here you need to ensure that your thesis runs in the order that is dictated by your individual institution. As I have said many times, you need to check that the style and format of your thesis is correct. I always tell my students to set up a 'Word template' in the format that the thesis is to appear in, so that it will have the correct margins, font and font size. Remember earlier in the book when I was discussing following instructions? This is what I was referring to: the written instructions set by your institution for the correct layout for the submission of the dissertation thesis, which is normally part of the marking criteria, usually under 'style'.

The margins will be largely dependent on the style of binding in which your institution wishes you to submit your thesis. For some institutions, spiral binding is now the norm. However, at one time (for undergraduates) the thesis had to be bound in black buckram, which meant that the left margin had to be large enough to accommodate this type of binding. Again, this information will be provided in the guidelines given to you by your institution. So be sure you are fully conversant with the layout and running order that the thesis needs to be in.

Copy-editing

Once you have completed the above task, you now need to move onto checking for consistency in your writing. For example, is the language you use throughout your dissertation consistent? Does the awarding institution, namely your university, require your references and citations in a particular format? Usually the referencing style is Harvard; however, in some countries the referencing style may be APA (American Psychological Association). For Harvard referencing I have found the following website very useful: http://libweb.anglia.ac.uk/referencing/ harvard.htm; for the APA 6th format, the University of Chester has a really easy guide to use; this can be found at http:// facultyhub.weebly.com/uploads/4/9/1/1/4911205/apa_2014.pdf. I have used both these styles throughout my studies but, having said this, I, like my students, have to comply with my own institution's guidelines on this (http://www.hud.ac.uk/library/ finding-info/apa-referencing/), as will you with your own university. Every institution is different, so check the guidelines carefully.

Diagrams and tables

I have touched upon this earlier in the book, but just to recap. The diagrams and tables must be numbered correctly and have titles. So, for example, if you use a diagram in Chapter 2, let us say Maslow's hierarchy of needs, and it is the first diagram in that chapter, it would appear as follows:

Fig. 2.1 Maslow's hierarchy of needs

If you produced a table of these needs with an explanation and, again, it was the first table in that chapter, it would appear as:

Table 2.1 Maslow's hierarchy of needs with explanations

All the tables and diagrams run consecutively, in each chapter. Furthermore, note that in each new chapter you would start at 1 again; for example, Fig. 3.1; Fig. 4.1. The first number denotes the chapter that the diagram or table is appearing in, and the second number tells us the order of the diagrams as they appear in the chapter. It is the same with the tables.

Pagination

What is this, I hear you ask! It is a posh word for page numbering. You will need to ensure that your pages are numbered correctly. Again, you will need to check your guidelines on where your university wishes you to place your page numbers and in what style. It is common for pages that appear in the thesis before Chapter 1 to carry Roman numerals, for example: i, ii, iii, iv, and so on. The first proper page, page 1 (one), is usually the first page of Chapter 1. So make sure you get this correct. You are marked for presentation and this is part of that criterion; it is also a good style to adopt. Look at any books and you will find this form of pagination.

Appendices

These are used when the material you have would disrupt the flow of your discussion; for example, any tables you have from other sources, or tables and graphs you have produced from your data that would be better placed here. Do not use the appendices to try to get around the word count; you should only include materials and artefacts relevant to your study, but which are too large to include in the main discussion.

Each artefact, table, or whatever should appear on a separate page, and each appendix should carry its own heading, for example, 'Appendix A' or 'Appendix 1'. It makes no difference whether you use numbers or letters, but you do need to be consistent and in line with your institution's requirements.

One final point on appendices: these should appear in the order as they appear in the thesis, and after your bibliography, not before.

Tables and lists

In your thesis, you will need to produce the following:

Table of Contents: this is where you will need to provide a list of the headings and sub-headings, and where they appear (page numbers).

List of Tables: this is where you will identify the pages where the tables appear.

List of Figures: like the list of tables, this lists where the figures that you have used appear.

List of Acronyms: it is good practice to incorporate this list, as it gives the reader an explanation and quick reference check as to what the acronyms stand for. Provide the full name followed by the acronym in brackets the first time it appears in the main text, then use the acronym only thereafter, for example: customer relationship marketing (CRM).

When you are editing and copy-editing, you will need to go back and check that these lists still hold true, as they might change if you delete anything, or move things around. I will not lie to you: this is a chore but a necessary task, so make sure you get it right.

Binding

I have discussed binding throughout this book. However, you need to be aware of what is called 'lead time'. This is the time needed by the binder to bind the individual copies of your thesis. Some students bind their work themselves, but remember there will be other students also wishing to have their copies bound professionally. Black buckram can take up to three weeks to bind, so you will need to build this into your work schedule.

Marking criteria

You should have a copy of this stuck to your wall next to your computer, so that you can very quickly check that you are meeting the criteria set by your institution. I always tell my students to go through the criteria and ensure that they can see where they may be awarded marks in each section. I also tell them to use some of the words in the criteria in their discussion section when they are evidencing how they have addressed particular objectives. Each section of your thesis will carry a weighting, and you should be aiming to get the best possible grade you can in each of these sections.

Submitting your work

The end is in sight! I can actually hear the huge sigh of relief and visualise the big smile emerging on your face.

One final check: make sure you submit the correct number of hard copies, and that you submit any electronic copies to such software that your institution uses to check for possible plagiarism.

Oh, and yes, for goodness sake, make sure you hand it in on time. The time and date of submitting your thesis should be etched in your brain.

There is no reason for any student to forget the hand-in date. Nevertheless, year on year, I hear this from some students.

Why produce all that hard work and then put yourself in the position where you might fail or be capped at 40% for being late in submitting your work.

Your 30-second recap

I've highlighted the level of 'craftsmanship' that's needed to finalise your thesis. I bet you weren't aware that so much work needed to be undertaken before you could submit, or should submit, your thesis!

You'll need to proofread your work, eliminating any errors you can find. Sometimes you'll find that you cannot see the wood for the trees. Step away from your work for about a day, and then come back to it with fresh eyes.

Remember to build the time for proofreading your work into your schedule, and for getting your copies bound professionally.

I've walked you through what you need to consider in terms of layout and reiterated that you must follow the guide set by your institution.

I've also provided you with some website addresses where you can obtain some guidance on Harvard and APA referencing.

Chapter 9: What happens next?

Introduction

Let me give you a brief insight of what happens to your thesis when you have submitted it and the process used to award you your final grade.

Reading

As you will no doubt be aware, there is a lot of reading that takes place by the academics who have supervised the dissertations. Remember, your supervisor may have anything up to 40 theses to read, then first mark or second mark. Yes, they do read your thesis; I for one can assure you that I do. However, you must remember that your supervisor also has other duties to perform, and any interruptions means breaking away from reading.

The supervisor has to work his or her way through your thesis, awarding marks against the criteria that have been set as they go along. They will then award you a provisional grade.

Grading

When your supervisor has undertaken the grading of your work, she or he then needs to wait for the second marker to complete the grading of your work. This is to remove any possible bias that may creep in from your supervisor when they marked and graded your work. This is the first quality control check. When both have finished marking, they will then get together to go through your work, discussing how they reached a grade for each section, and the final overall grade. Some of these debates can be quick, as the markers may have awarded the same grade, or it could be lengthy, as they may have different opinions. In this case, they will need to agree on a final grade. Sometimes agreement cannot be found, and in this instance it has to go to a third marker, who will mark it without knowledge of the first two grades awarded. After marking it, the third marker's grade is the one that will stand. This grade will count towards your final qualification. As a final quality control check with instances such as this, the thesis will also be sent to the external examiner for final checking.

After this procedure, a selection of theses are grouped together from each category (including those that have been third-marked); that is, some from the 70+ grade, some from the 60-69 grade, some from the 50-59 grade, and some from the 40-49 grade. These selected theses, together with those awarded a fail grade, are sent to the 'external examiner' (a lecturer from another university). This lecturer (and there are others, undertaking this task at the same time, in different specialisations at different universities) will go through them to ensure that the theses have been marked in compliance with the guidelines and policies set by the awarding body, and that the grade awarded is an accurate reflection of the criteria set. Sometimes institutions wait until the exam boards, and then provide all the external examiners with a quiet room where they go through the theses and rubber stamp the grade awarded, or comment on certain dissertations at the exam board for those present to consider.

It's all over

Once your grade as been internally moderated and externally agreed, you can now sit back and wait for the day when you graduate. You should be proud of what you have achieved. You have come a long way and I hope you have attained the grade you deserve. Remember, you will only get out of the exercise what you put in to it. It is hard work, but you will have proven that you can do it. Well done!

Bibliography

Adcock, C. J., 1989. Pre-Sampling Procedures. *The Statistician*, 38 (2), pp.107-115.

Amaratunga, D., Baldry, D., Sarshar, M. & Newton, R., 2002. Quantitative and Qualitative Research in the Built Environment: application of "Mixed" Research Approach. *Works Study*, 51 (1), pp.17-31.

Aunger, R., 1995. On Ethnography: Story Telling or Science? *Current Anthropology*, 36 (1), pp.97-130.

Aveyard, H., 2010. Doing a Literature Review in Health and Social Care. Maidenhead, Open University Press.

BERA, 2004. *Revised Ethical Guidelines for Educational Research (2004)*. Available at: www.bera.ac.uk/publications/pdfs/ETHICAL1.pdf [Accessed 13 January 2008].

Bhardwaj, M. & Monin, J., 2006. Tacit to Explicit: An Interplay Shaping Organization Knowledge. *Journal of Knowledge Management*, 10 (3), pp.72-85.

Boch, F. & Piolat, A., 2005. Note Taking and Learning: A Summary of Research. *The WAC Journal*, 16, pp.101-113.

Booth, C. & Harrington, J., 2003. Research Methods Modules and Undergraduate Business Research: An Investigation. *International Journal of Management Education*, 3 (3), pp. 19-31.

Bordens, K. S. & Abbott, B. B., 2005. Research Design and Methods – A Process Approach. 6th ed. New York, McGraw-Hill Companies.

Bryman, A., 2008. *Social Research Methods*, 3rd ed. Oxford, Oxford University Press.

Check, J. & Schutt, R. K., 2012. *Research Methods in Education*. California, SAGE Publications Inc.

Clark, A. M., 1998. The Qualitative – Quantitative Debate: Moving from Positivism and Confrontation to Post-Positivism and Reconciliation. *Journal of Advanced Nursing*, 27, pp. 1242-1249.

Cochran, W. G., Mosteller, F. & Tukey, J. W., 1954. Principles of Sampling. *Journal of the American Statistical Association*, 49 (265), pp.13-35.

Cohen, L., Manion, L. & Morrison, K., 2000. *Research Methods in Education*. 5th ed. London, Routledge Falmer.

Creswell, J. W., 2009. Research Design – Qualitative, Quantitative, and Mixed Methods Approaches. 3rd ed. California, SAGE Publications Inc.

Cummings, L., 1998. The Scientific Reductionism of Relevance Theory: The Lesson from Logical Positivism. *Journal of Pragmatics*, 29, pp.1-12.

Dawson, C., 2009. Introduction to Research Methods – A Practical Guide for Anyone Undertaking a Research Project. 4th ed. Begbroke, How To Books Limited.

de Vaus, D., 2003. *Research Design in Social Research*. London, SAGE Publications Limited.

Denzin, N. K., 2003. The Practices and Politics of Interpretation. *In*: Denzin, N. K. & Lincoln, Y. S. (eds.) *Collecting and Interpreting Qualitative Materials*. 2nd ed. Series London: SAGE Publications Limited, pp.458-498.

Denzin, N. K. & Lincoln, Y. S., 2003. Introduction: The Discipline and Practice of Qualitative Research. In: N. K. Denzin & Y. S.

Lincoln, eds. *Collecting and Interpreting Qualitative Materials*. 2nd ed. Series. London: SAGE Publications Limited, pp.1-46.

Easterby-Smith, M., Thorpe, R. & Lowe, A., 2004. *Management Research – An Introduction*. 2nd ed. London, SAGE Publications Limited.

Elton, L., 2010. Academic Writing and Tacit Knowledge. *Teaching in Higher Education*, 15 (2), pp.151-160.

Feather, D., 2004. The Teaching of Higher Education in Further Education: Academic Identities in Business Studies Departments, School of Education and Professional Development, University of Huddersfield, Proposal for Doctorate.

Feather, D., 2009. *Academic Identities: Voices from the Edge*. Doctor of Education [Doctoral Thesis], The Business School, University of Huddersfield.

Feather, D., 2010. A Whisper of Academic Identity: An HE in FE Perspective. *Research in Post-Compulsory Education*, 15 (2), pp. 189-204.

Field, A., 2009. *Discovering Statistics using SPSS*. 3rd ed. London, SAGE Publications Limited.

Fowler Junior, F. J., 1992. How Unclear Terms Affect Survey Data. *The Public Opinion Quarterly*, 56 (2), pp.218-231.

Garner, M., 2012. *There's madness in our methods: The pedagogical culture of research methods*. HEA Social Sciences Teaching and Learning Summit: Teaching Research Methods, 21-22 June 2012 Radcliffe House, University of Warwick. York: The Higher Education Academy – Social Sciences, 1-10, Available at:
www.heacademy.ac.uk/assets/documents/events/ss_assets/Blog/Garner_fullpaper.pdf [Accessed 10 October 2012].

Glaser, B. G. & Strauss, A. L., 1999. The Discovery of Grounded Theory: Strategies for Qualitative Research. New Jersey, Aldine Transaction.

Gray, D. E., 2009. *Doing Research in the Real World*. 2nd ed. London, SAGE Publications Limited.

Habermass, J., 1987. *Knowledge and Human Interests*. Translated by: Shapiro, J. J. Cambridge, Polity Press.

Hart, C., 2008. Doing a Literature Review – Releasing the Social Science Research Imagination. London, SAGE Publications Limited.

Hennink, M., Hutter, I. & Bailey, A., 2011. *Qualitative Research Methods*. London, SAGE Publications Limited.

Huddersfield University Ethics Committee, 2005. *University of Huddersfield Ethical Guidelines for Good Practice in Teaching and Research*. Available at: http://www2.hud.ac.uk/shared/shared_rwg/documents/vgc_regulations/ethical_guidelines.pdf [Accessed 10 August 2010].

Jackson, H., 2009. *Writing the Proposal – Lecture Slides, Strategy and Marketing*. University of Huddersfield. Management Research Workshop. Available at: http://virtual.hud.ac.uk [Accessed 9 June 2010].

Jankowicz, A. D., 2007. *Business Research Projects*. 3rd ed. London, Thomson Learning.

LeCompte, M. D., 2000. Analyzing Qualitative Data. *Theory Into Practice*, 39 (3), pp.146-154.

Maylor, H. & Blackmon, K., 2005. Researching Business and Management. New York, Palgrave MacMillan.

Moran, D. & Mooney, T. (eds.), 2002. *The Phenomenology Reader*, London, Routledge.

Oliver, P., 2010. *Understanding the Research Process*. London, SAGE Publications Limited.

Oppenheim, A. N., 2001. Questionnaire Design, Interviewing and Attitude Measurement. New ed. London, Continuum.

Quinlan, C., 2011. *Business Research Methods*. Andover, South-Western Cengage Learning.

QUT, 2008. *QUT Referencing and Notetaking Templates*. Available at: http://www.citewrite.qut.edu.au/about/QUTcitewrite-2010_templates.pdf [Accessed 2 January 2013].

Ridley, D., 2012. The Literature Review Process – A Step-by-Step Guide for Students. London, SAGE Publications Limited.

Roberts, C. M., 2010. The Dissertation Journey – A Practical and Comprehensive Guide to Planning, Writing, and Defending Your Dissertation. 2nd ed. California, Corwin.

Robson, C., 2002. *Real World Research*. 2nd ed. Oxford, Blackwell Publishing.

Rolfe, G., 2006. Validity, Trustworthiness and Rigour: Quality and the Idea of Qualitative Research. *Journal of Advanced Nursing*, 56 (3), pp.304-310.

Ryan, G. W. & Bernard, H. R., 2003. Data Management and Analysis Methods. In: N. K. Denzin & Y. S. Lincoln, eds. *Collecting and Interpreting Qualitative Materials*. 2nd ed. Series London: SAGE Publications Limited, pp.259-309.

Saunders, M., Lewis, P. & Thornhill, A., 2007. *Research Methods for Business Students*. 4th ed. Harlow, Pearson Education Limited.

Saunders, M., Lewis, P. & Thornhill, A., 2009. *Research Methods for Business Students*. 5th ed. Harlow, Pearson Education Limited.

Sekaran, U. & Bougie, R., 2009. Research Methods for Business – A Skill Building Approach. 5th ed. Chichester, John Wiley & Sons Limited.

Silverman, D., 2002. Interpreting Qualitative Data – Methods for Analysing Talk, Text and Interaction. 2nd ed. London, SAGE Publications Limited.

Smeyers, P., 2001. Qualitative Versus Quantitative Design: A Plea for a Paradigmatic Tolerance in Education Research. *Journal of Philosophy of Education*, 35 (3), pp.478-495.

Smith, J. A., Flowers, P. & Larking, M., 2009. Interpretative Phenomenological Analysis Theory, Method and Research. London, SAGE Publications Limited.

Spradley, J. P., 1979. *The Ethnographic Interview*. Belmont CA, USA, Wadsworth Group/Thomson Learning.

Strauss, A. L., 2003. Qualitative Analysis for Social Scientists. Cambridge, Cambridge University Press.

Swetnam, D., 2000. Writing Your Dissertation – How to Plan, Prepare and Present Successful Work. Oxford, How To Books Limited.

Teddlie, C. & Tashakkori, A., 2009. Foundations of Mixed Methods Research – Integrating Quantitative and Qualitative Approaches in the Social and Behavioral Sciences. California, SAGE Publications Inc.

Thomas, J. R., Nelson, J. K. & Silverman, S. J., 2011. *Research Methods in Physical Activity*. 6th ed. Champaign, Human Kinetics.

Torgerson, D. J. & Torgerson, C. J., 2003. Avoiding Bias in Randomised Controlled Trials in Education Research. *British Journal of Educational Studies*, 51 (1), pp.36-45.

Walcott, H. F., 2001. *Writing up Qualitative Research*. 2nd ed. California, SAGE Publications Inc.

Wallace, M. & Wray, A., 2011. Critical Reading and Writing for Postgraduates. 2nd ed. London, SAGE Publications Limited.

Walliman, N., 2005. Your Undergraduate Dissertation – The Essential Guide for Success. London. California, SAGE Publications Inc.

White, B., 2000. Dissertation Skills for Business and Management Students. London, Cengage Learning.

Williams, M., 2000. Interpretivism and Generalisation. *Sociology*, 34 (2), pp.209-224.

References

Buckingham, A. & Saunders, P., 2004. The survey methods workbook – from design to analysis. Cambridge, Polity Press.

Charmaz, K., 2014. *Constructing grounded theory*. 2nd ed. London, Sage Publications.

Clough, P. & Nutbrown, C., 2012. *A Student's Guide to Methodology*. 3rd ed. London, Sage Publishers.

Feather, D., 2009. *Academic Identities: Voices from the Edge*. Doctor of Education, The Business School, University of Huddersfield.

Forshaw, M., 2012. *Critical Thinking for Psychology – A Student Guide*. Chichester, British Psychological Society and John Wiley and Sons.

Freshwater, D. & Cahill, J., 2013. Paradigms lost and paradigms regained. *Journal of Mixed Methods Research,* 7 (1), pp.3-5.

Mertens, D. M., 2012. What comes first? The paradigm or the approach? *Journal of Mixed Methods Research,* 6 (4), pp.255-257.

Mullins, L. J., 2006. *Essentials of Organisational Behaviour,* 8th ed. Harlow, Pearson Education Limited.

Oppenheim, A. N., 2001. Questionnaire Design, Interviewing and Attitude Measurement. New ed. London, Continuum.

Osmond, A., 2013. Academic writing and grammar for students. London, Sage Publications.

Roberts, C. M., 2010. The Dissertation Journey - A practical and comprehensive guide to planning, writing, and defending your dissertation. 2nd ed. California, Corwin.

Rollinson, D., 2005. Organisational Behaviour Analysis: An Integrated Approach. 3rd ed. Harlow, Pearson Education Limited.

Silverman, D., 2002. Interpreting Qualitative Data – Methods for Analysing Talk, Text and Interaction. 2nd ed. London, Sage Publications Limited.

Teddlie, C. & Tashakkori, A., 2009. Foundations of mixed methods research. London, Sage Publications.

Wray, K. B., 2011. Kuhn and the discovery of paradigms. *Philosophy of the Social Sciences,* 41 (3), pp.380-397.

Other titles from White & MacLean Publishing:

From Comfort Zone to Performance Management
by Alasdair White

This book seeks to take the established behavioural models relating to comfort zones, group and individual development, and managing change, and use them to create a methodology for understanding and managing performance. It seeks to provide a reliable approach to getting the best out of people that is firmly based on sound behavioural and psychological principles backed up by observational data and practical field research. It is not, however, a 'scientific' paper full of detailed research data, complex theories and high-flown rhetoric, but rather it is a practical guide based on twenty years of consultancy in the field and eight years of teaching university students in a business school.

In understanding and managing performance, the key is the management of the stress. Both motivation and anxiety are, behaviourally, sub-sets of stress and, consequently, they are tools to assist in performance management – there will be times when motivation will be the most useful tool, while at others the introduction of anxiety will be more appropriate. However, too much motivation or anxiety will result in too much stress and this will result in performance being disabled.

The correct management style needs to be applied in each phase if performance is to be maximised. Applying the incorrect style has a negative impact on performance. In situations in which a series of performance-enhancing steps need to be taken, it is imperative to start the new performance cycle at the point at which the old performance cycle develops a slowing performance trend.

From Comfort Zone to Performance Management is available as an eBook. To order go to:
www.whiteandmaclean.eu/from-comfort-zone-to-performance-management/

Managing for Performance
by Alasdair White

Performance management is crucial to a manager's success. To be an effective manager you need to concentrate on three main areas of responsibility: determining the objective of your team and how it will be reached; ensuring your team members are selected, developed and trained appropriately; and motivating the individuals so that the objective is achieved.

Managing for Performance is an accessible, practical guide to performance management techniques and how to apply them. Chapters look at how to manage upwards in order to achieve the objective, planning and resources, you and your management style, communicating information, selling the cause, setting goals, and monitoring performance and feedback. With the help of illuminating examples, Alasdair White enables you to obtain the best performance possible from yourself and your team so that you fulfil all of your aims and goals.

Managing for Performance will appeal to all managers who want to improve their leadership skills and increase the efficiency of their team.

First published by Piatkus Books in 1995, this edition of *Managing for Performance* is available as an eBook. To order or to read a sample chapter, go to:
www.whiteandmaclean.eu/managing-for-performance-ebook/

Some fiction titles:

Shadows
by Alex Hunter

Following the murder of a young investigative journalist in France, Luc Hansen, an ex-Legionnaire now working for the elite but shadowy DER, the European Union's security and intelligence directorate, uncovers a massive fraud within the European Commission in Brussels. But his investigation is endangered and the life of his partner, Joanna Donnelly, threatened by the existence of a 'mole' high inside the DER itself.

As he tracks the money flow from Brussels through London to Prague, he discovers it is being used to send guns to the Sunni militias fighting the US forces in Iraq and to the Kurdish separatists. Still unable to prove exactly who is involved, Luc travels to Iraq where the militia captures him. In a daring escape, he makes his way north to the Kurdish area in the Zagros Mountains and assists them in destroying the power of the militia in the area.

Back in Belgium, Luc embarks on a new strategy to force his opponents into the open in a desperate race to close down the arms route and arrest those involved. Luc and his team find themselves in extreme danger, culminating in a fierce gun battle deep in the Belgian countryside, the outcome of which hangs in the balance.

Shadows is available as a paperback and as an eBook. To order or to read a sample chapter and to listen to an interview with the author, go to: www.whiteandmaclean.eu/shadows/

Praise for *Shadows*:

SHADOWS is a real page-turner as its taut style, rapid pace and gradual heightening of tension keeps the reader wanting to discover – 'What next?' The characters develop with the same controlled economy of language and the combination of an ingenious plot and believable characters makes this a thoroughly good read. I would hope to meet Luc and Joanna again!
GH Belgium

SHADOWS 'gets one in' right from the prologue, and seemingly effortlessly keeps the reader turning the pages to find out what happens next. Fast paced, like the world that unfolds in the story, the characters are real and the plot just a little too believable. As I was reading, I actually asked myself: has Alex Hunter strayed too near the truth!
HM Hong Kong

Retribution

by Alex Hunter

No one saw who threw the fire-bomb. It arched over the crowd, hit the lights on the top of the police car, broke and sent burning fuel over the vehicle. A deep collective sigh went up from those at the front of the crowd, but no one moved as the police driver and his partner scrambled to safety.

In the oppressive heat of summer, Luc Hansen, a senior agent in the European Union's security and intelligence directorate, uncovers a covert CIA operation in which a neo-con group of ageing Americans are fomenting ethnic unrest in Europe and are willing to use Predator drones and nerve gas against Syrian civilians in an attempt to force their Iranian nemesis to Europe so that they can kill him. In a shadowy world in which different versions of the truth exist, all communications are compromised and no one is quite who they seem, Hansen has to use all his skills just to stay alive.

Retribution is available as a paperback and as an eBook. To order or to read a sample chapter, go to: www.whiteandmaclean.eu/retribution/

Praise for *Retribution*:

I didn't put it down until I got to the end! A thriller it is indeed and a very gripping one. I was pleased to find myself with Hansen and Donnelly again, and Ariana is a lovable character.

AS Paris

The cover is stunning and demanded to be read – I had to tear myself away or nothing planned for today would have got done.

RH Dublin

I read RETRIBUTION in a couple of days, staying up late, continually seeking to finish chapters to find out what happens next. Well done! Overall, it's a wonderful read, and I thoroughly enjoyed myself.

RS Hong Kong

www.whiteandmaclean.eu